"Deep, rich, and nourishing—*Joseph* is vintage Lennox. He has the rare gift of opening life as well as the biblical text, so that we come away understanding God's ways more clearly and trusting him more fully."

Os Guinness, author, *The Call*

"I thought I really knew the story of Joseph—but was thrilled by the fact that in chapter after chapter, there were so many fresh insights. If you don't believe me, just turn to the chapter on Joseph and Potiphar's wife. John Lennox has written a riveting commentary on one of the timeless characters of the Bible."

Rico Tice, Senior Minister (Evangelism), All Souls Church, London

"You may think this story is familiar, but again and again Lennox brings forth new gems in this expert guide through Joseph's dysfunctional family history. Despite the depth of tragedy, God brought hope."

Peter J. Williams, Principal, Tyndale House, Cambridge

"*Joseph* is a powerful word for us today. Joseph is tested and trained through suffering and broken relationships to become a forgiving brother, son, and leader, and his relationship with God is not only a stabilizing factor but a sustaining force in his life. Throughout the book, we see how a man with a transformative relationship with God can be used by God in all areas of his life: family, work, bondage, business, government, and faith. Lennox skillfully looks back to the ancestors of Joseph to show how history was repeating in his family, and he looks forward to the life of Jesus to give us hope."

Bob Shettler, Pastor, First Presbyterian Church, Gainesville, Florida

"John Lennox, a renowned scientist and Oxford professor, is also a remarkable, gifted expositor and Bible teacher. I had the pleasure of hearing this material when it was initially presented to a large group of European leaders, and I heartily commend it. The deep spiritual understanding and careful research that Lennox brings to Joseph's story will bring rich dividends to the reader."

Luder G. Whitlock Jr., Executive Director, CNL Charitable Foundation, Inc.; Former President and Professor Emeritus, Reformed Theological Seminary; author, *Divided We Fall* and *The Spiritual Quest*

T0373358

Joseph

Joseph

A Story of Love, Hate, Slavery,
Power, and Forgiveness

John C. Lennox

WHEATON, ILLINOIS

Cover design: Jeff Miller, Faceout Studios

Cover image: Thevenin, Charles (1764–1838) / Joseph Recognised by his Brothers, 1789 / Bridgeman Images

First printing 2019

Printed in the United States of America

Scripture quotations are from the ESV® Bible (The Holy Bible, English Standard Version®), copyright © 2001 by Crossway, a publishing ministry of Good News Publishers. Used by permission. All rights reserved.

All emphases in Scripture quotations have been added by the author.

Trade paperback ISBN: 978-1-4335-6293-8
ePub ISBN: 978-1-4335-6296-9
PDF ISBN: 978-1-4335-6294-5
Mobipocket ISBN: 978-1-4335-6295-2

Library of Congress Cataloging-in-Publication Data

Names: Lennox, John C., 1943- author.
Title: Joseph : a story of love, hate, slavery, power, and forgiveness / John C. Lennox.
Description: Wheaton : Crossway, 2019. | Includes bibliographical references and index.
Identifiers: LCCN 2018042368 (print) | LCCN 2018054419 (ebook) | ISBN 9781433562945 (pdf) | ISBN 9781433562952 (mobi) | ISBN 9781433562969 (epub) | ISBN 9781433562938 (tp)
Subjects: LCSH: Joseph (Son of Jacob)
Classification: LCC BS580.J6 (ebook) | LCC BS580.J6 L465 2019 (print) | DDC 222/.11092—dc23
LC record available at https://lccn.loc.gov/2018042368

Crossway is a publishing ministry of Good News Publishers.

Contents

Introduction

The story of Joseph the son of Jacob has a timeless quality that is undiminished in its capacity to probe the depths, the heights, the sorrows, and the joys that form the intricate tapestry of relationships between men and women and their engagement with God.

In broad strokes, this story, familiar to many people from childhood, tracks the complex path of Joseph's extraordinary life from his early days in a rather dysfunctional family—on the one hand, enjoying his father's favoritism, as indicated by the famous coat of many colors; and, on the other hand, in consequence of that favoritism, enduring his brothers' increasingly hurtful taunts and bullying. His strange dreams that cast him in the role of leader in his family inflame his brothers' hatred to the point where they determine to murder him when they see him coming to visit them as they tend cattle far from home.

At the last moment fratricide is narrowly avoided when one of the brothers, Judah, suggests that Joseph be sold to a passing caravan of Midianite slave traffickers. The deal done, Joseph is taken to Egypt where he is sold as a domestic slave to Potiphar, a senior official in Pharaoh's retinue.[1] Joseph proves himself an outstanding house steward and is soon entrusted with running Potiphar's entire domestic economy. However, Joseph becomes

---

1. The word *pharaoh* is the Greek form of the Egyptian *pero* or *per-a-a*, which was the designation for the royal residence and means "Great House." The name of the residence became associated with the ruler and, in time, was used exclusively for the leader of the people.

the focus of Potiphar's wife's desires and, when he rejects her advances, she denounces him to Potiphar, who throws Joseph into prison without a hearing.

Yet even when unjustly incarcerated, Joseph's administrative skills are put to use, and it is not long before he becomes the trusted administrator of the prison under its director. Nothing much happens until, eventually, two state prisoners are put in his care, Pharaoh's cupbearer and his baker. They have dreams that they share with Joseph, who correctly interprets them as indicating that the former will be restored to his position and the latter will be executed. Joseph takes the opportunity to explain his own false arrest and incarceration to the cupbearer and asks him on his release to mention him favorably to Pharaoh. However, the cupbearer forgets Joseph for the next two years, recalling him only when Pharaoh himself has disturbing dreams.

Pharaoh summons Joseph, who interprets Pharaoh's dreams as a message from God that Egypt is about to enjoy seven years of plenty followed by seven years of severe famine. In light of this, Joseph advises that Pharaoh should organize the food supplies for the nation. Pharaoh perceives the wisdom in Joseph's detailed economic advice and at once makes him Egypt's grand vizier and minister of agriculture, second only in national ranking to Pharaoh himself.

Joseph, catapulted from prison to high office of state, at once sets about using his consummate administrative skill and his new powers to set up vast storehouses for the nation's grain. This system works so well that the Egyptian granary storehouses are full to overflowing by the end of the years of plenty.

Then come the years of famine as foreseen in Pharaoh's dreams. The shortage of food affects not only Egypt but also the surrounding nations that are forced to come to Egypt for food aid. Among those who come for help are Joseph's brothers, who arrive at a distribution center overseen by Joseph himself. They fail to recognize him although he recognizes them.

The scene is now set for a fascinating and complex human drama in which Joseph, as yet unrecognized by his brothers, uses his power and influence behind the scenes to awaken their consciences to face what they have done. Eventually, when he is convinced that they have repented, he reveals himself to them and publicly forgives and embraces them in one of the most moving scenes in all of world literature.

It is a masterpiece of storytelling. Elegant use of simple, flowing language carries us into a world that seems at first glance utterly removed from our world, and yet, as we think our way into the narrative, it rapidly becomes a penetrating searchlight into the complex psychodramas of our own lives.

Joseph's story has inspired great literature, for instance, German author Thomas Mann's four-part novel *Joseph and his Brothers*, often regarded as one of Mann's greatest literary achievements. It has inspired great art, such as F. Overbeck's depiction of Joseph being sold by his brothers; Giovanni Andrea de Ferrari's powerful representation of Joseph's blood-sprinkled coat being shown to his distraught father Jacob; Philipp Veit's rendering of Joseph fleeing from Potiphar's wife; and, perhaps most famous of all, Rembrandt's painting of Jacob as an old man blessing Joseph's second son in preference to Joseph's firstborn.

It is a story about two cultures—the nomadic culture of Canaan where Joseph spends his first seventeen years, and the high civilization of Egypt where he spends the rest of his life. In this and many other respects Joseph's story parallels that of Daniel. Daniel's first fifteen years or so were spent in the small tribal state of Judah and the rest of his life in the high civilization of Babylon. Both men started off as captives and eventually rose to similarly high office in the administration of their respective countries of exile. But there is a very important difference between them. Joseph entered Egypt as a slave to a powerful military man, whereas Daniel, though a captive, was enrolled in the university at Babylon in order to study the culture, language, and laws and enter on a career of administration. There is no record of Joseph receiving any formal education, although it is not impossible.

There are six major empires that bestride biblical history: Egypt, Assyria, Babylon, Medo-Persia, Greece, and Rome. Joseph plays a major role in the first, Daniel in the third. Central to those roles was their gift for interpreting dreams.

The relevance of the culture and ideology of polytheistic Babylon to the book of Daniel is fairly easy to see, as I have tried to explain elsewhere.[2] We shall have to work harder to see the relevance of the culture of similarly polytheistic Egypt to the story of Joseph, but it is there nonetheless.

The account of Joseph's life occupies the final movement of the book of Genesis. It begins quite abruptly in Genesis 37:2: "These are the generations of Jacob. Joseph, being seventeen years old, was pasturing the flock with his brothers." This phrase, "These are the generations of," occurs several times in Genesis and is well recognized as a literary marker that the author of the book uses to divide his long narrative into its major movements.

The emphasis at this point on Jacob and not only Joseph reminds us that this final section of Genesis is not simply the story of Joseph. It is still to be seen as the story of Jacob. In fact, though the book ends with the death of Joseph, the death of Jacob is recorded in the penultimate chapter. Nor is it simply the story of Joseph and Jacob. It is properly to be seen as the story of Jacob and his sons—the "generations of Jacob." Joseph's destiny is inextricably entwined with that of his many brothers.

2. John C. Lennox, *Against the Flow: The Inspiration of Daniel in an Age of Relativism* (Oxford, UK: Lion Hudson, 2015).

PART 1

THE BROADER CONTEXT IN GENESIS

1

The Structure of Genesis

Complex lives have complex backgrounds, and Joseph's is no exception, so, before we start to think about the detail of the Joseph narrative, we need to step back and set it in the context of the rest of the book of Genesis in order to give depth to our understanding. Since the narrative of Joseph's life comes at the end of Genesis, that background is considerable. My view is that the Genesis background enriches the story considerably since the book is a unity. After all, the author of Genesis anticipates that you read all of the book and not just the last part.

As is the custom in that part of the world, Joseph would have grown up on a diet of stories of the great heroes of Israel's tribal history. He would have been steeped in the fascinating narratives of his father, Jacob, his grandfather Isaac, and his great-grandfather Abraham. But not only that—he would have been acquainted with their prehistory right back to the beginning. In other words, he would have known a good deal of the plotline of the book of Genesis, so it is there that we must begin, for we need to know some of what Joseph knew.

Genesis is more than a narrative. It is a metanarrative giving us a grand framework for our understanding of the universe and life.

In order to grasp its story—Genesis is, after all, a large book—it is helpful to have some idea of its literary shape. It turns out that the author uses a simple literary device in order to structure his material, the repetition at intervals of the phrase: "These are the generations of . . ." (the phrase occurs at 2:4; 5:1; 6:9; 10:1; 11:10, 27; 25:12, 19; 36:1; 37:2). The six main sections the phrase indicates are: 1:1–2:4; 2:5–4:26; 5:1–9:29; 10:1–25:11; 25:12–35:29; and 36:1–50:26. Several of the sections have more than one instance of the repeated phrase in order to delineate subsections.

The first part of the book consists of three sections that record the creation of human beings in the image of God. The second part of the book consists of three sections that cover the lives of the patriarchs. The first section in the second part ends with the death of Abraham, the second section with the death of Isaac, and the third section with the deaths of Jacob and Joseph.

Above all, Genesis tells us about the God in whom Joseph believed, the God he learned to trust.

Section 1: Creation (Genesis 1:1–2:3)

The book begins with the origin of the universe in the mind and creative energy of God: "In the beginning, God created the heavens and the earth" (1:1). This first majestic sentence undergirds and gives meaning to the developing saga that follows. It asserts that the universe we inhabit is a creation. The world did not generate itself. It did not spring into being spontaneously from nothing. God caused it to be.

By asserting the existence of a Creator, the opening words of Genesis constitute a frontal attack on the materialist atheist philosophy that dominates so much of the Western world today. That philosophy has a long history reaching back beyond the atomism of the ancient Greek thinkers Democritus and Leucippus to the essentially materialistic theogonies of the ancient Near East—the birthplace of the Genesis story.

The book of Genesis was penned long before the ancient Greek philosophers had begun to formulate the ideas that are typically taken to represent the beginnings of philosophy. The lofty monotheism of the ancient Hebrews predates the Greek philosophers by centuries, a fact that is often lost in the current attempt to validate naturalism or materialism as the only worldview that holds intellectual credibility. Furthermore, in contradistinction to the Greeks, the Hebrew thinkers did not have to purge their worldview of a pantheon of god-projections of the forces of nature for the simple reason that they never did believe in such gods in the first place. The God of the Hebrews was not a projection of any force of nature. He was the Creator without whom there would be no forces, or, indeed, any nature in the first place.

The current naive trend of dismissing the God of the Bible as just another of the ancient mythical gods completely fails to grasp this distinction. Werner Jaeger, an expert on the gods of the ancient Near East, makes the point that those gods were descended from the heavens and the earth whereas the God of the Bible created the heavens and the earth. This holds in particular for the gods of the land of Egypt, where Joseph spent most of his life.

This briefest of brief histories of time opens with an elegant and fast-flowing account of the creation of the universe and of life in all its marvelous variety. The creation and organization of the cosmos proceeds in a series of steps, each of which is initiated by God speaking: "And God said . . ." These creative speech acts are summed up in the opening statement of the Gospel of John: "In the beginning was the Word, and the Word was with God, and the Word was God. . . . All things were made through him" (John 1:1, 3). This is the way things are. The Word is primary; the material universe is derivative and not the other way around, as popular secularism imagines.[1]

---

1. For more detail from both a biblical and a scientific perspective see my *Seven Days That Divide the World: The Beginning according to Genesis and Science* (Grand Rapids, MI: Zondervan, 2011).

The final step that climaxes the sequence is God's creation of human beings in his own image. Though the heavens reflect the glory of God, human beings are made in God's image. Only humans are. Humanity is unique.

Just what being made in the image of God means and how special human beings are is gradually revealed as an integral part of the biblical storyline. However, several very important aspects of that "image" are communicated in the early chapters of Genesis. The first is that after the sequence of repetitions of the phrase "And God said," we read something strikingly different: "And God said *to them*: Be fruitful and multiply" (1:28). Human beings are the kind of creature that God can speak to. They can hear and understand his words—and respond to them. It is that verbal relationship that is central to the biblical storyline.

Section 2: Human Life and Death (Genesis 2:4–4:26)

In the second major section we are told much more about the nature of human life. Human beings have a material substrate— they are made of the dust of the ground. They possess an aesthetic sense; they live in a world whose trees have been created good to look upon. They inhabit an environment that they can both cultivate and explore. They can enjoy that special relationship between man and woman, a relationship of beings created with equal status but as complementary rather than identical.

With deft strokes the author builds up a picture of the various features that make human life remarkable. But there is one more feature yet to be mentioned. It is by far the most important and, once again, it has to do with the word of God. It is that God spoke to the humans about the nature of life in the garden. He gave them permission to eat of every tree in the garden except for one: the tree of the knowledge of good and evil. This tree was in the middle of the garden, along with another special tree, the tree of life, to which they also had free access. Of the tree of the knowledge of good and evil God said: "In the day that you eat of it you shall surely die" (2:17).

There is much discussion among scholars as to the status and meaning of this portion of the story, and I must refer the reader to them for their comments. I wish to concentrate on what is often missed in such discussions: what the story is actually saying. For here we have a very clear, simple yet profound statement of the essence of morality—what it means to be a moral being. And morality is at the heart of the Joseph narrative.

First, the origin of morality, like the origin of the universe and of humanity, is to be found in God. This immediately brings to mind the famous statement of the Russian novelist Fyodor Dostoyevsky in *The Brothers Karamazov*: "If God does not exist, then everything is permissible."[2] Dostoyevsky was not, of course, suggesting that atheists are incapable of moral behavior. That would be a slanderous lie. After all, from the biblical perspective, all human beings are made in the image of God and so are moral beings, whether they believe in God or not. Hence atheists (or anyone else) can put others to shame by the quality of their moral behavior. Dostoyevsky was suggesting that there is no rational basis for morality if God does not exist, an issue that is as hotly debated today as is the parallel question of whether the universe itself is a creation of God or not. This book is not the right place to debate either of those issues.[3]

What is important here is that morality involves the capacity to decide whether to obey an injunction. Genesis here traces the moral order to God, who placed the first humans in a garden and gave them permission to eat from all the trees in that garden with one exception—the tree of the knowledge of good and evil.

It is obvious that the command not to eat the fruit of the tree of the knowledge of good and evil would have been meaningless

2. Fyodor Dostoyevsky, *The Brothers Karamozov*, trans. Richard Pevear and Larissa Volokhonsky (San Francisco: North Point Press, 1990), 589.
3. See my *Gunning for God: Why the New Atheists Are Missing the Target* (Oxford, UK: Lion Hudson, 2011).

if humans were not free to eat it. Thus, although human beings are clearly restricted in innumerable ways (they are not free, for instance, to run at 100 miles per hour), it is surely evident that they were not created as predetermined robots. They had real choice; they could choose to obey or disobey God's word, to eat or refrain from eating the forbidden fruit. This capacity to choose between alternatives is often described (somewhat misleadingly) as "libertarian freedom."

This Genesis account goes to the heart of the age-old complex and often impassioned debate about determinism and free will or the parallel, though not completely identical, debate about the relationship between the sovereignty of God and human responsibility.[4] It is to be noted that there are two separate questions here:

1. Does Scripture teach both that God rules and that humans have a certain degree of freedom?
2. If the answer is yes, how can this be so?

If we do not distinguish between these questions, there is a danger that failure to find a satisfactory answer to question 2 leads to reluctance to answer question 1 in the affirmative. This response is somewhat strange since there are many things in nature that we do not understand completely. For instance, it is well accepted by scientists that light behaves both like particles and waves. Understanding exactly *how* this works is another matter entirely.

We should note in passing that the assumption that human freedom is part of human dignity lies at the heart of all civilized societies. This is evidenced by the fact that such societies hold human beings responsible and answerable for their actions, hence the existence of legal institutions and procedures for law enforcement.

The analogy from science cited above may suggest a possible approach to the question of divine sovereignty and human freedom, and that is to see how they actually work out in the details

---

4. For an extended treatment of these topics see my *Determined to Believe?: The Sovereignty of God, Freedom, Faith, and Human Responsibility* (Oxford, UK: Lion Hudson, 2017).

of everyday life as recorded in Scripture. It is no accident that in connection with this issue the New Testament directs our attention specifically to the latter part of Genesis and the accounts of Isaac, Jacob, and their sons (see Romans 9–11). It will, therefore, be part of our story.

More in due course. For now the important thing to grasp is that the central feature of morality as described in the Genesis account is that it focuses on obedience to the word of God. By this, I mean that the humans had only God's word to tell them that eating the fruit from the tree of the knowledge of good and evil was potentially lethal. So the key question for them was simply this: Were they prepared to trust God's word? That was the thrust of the Serpent's temptation: "Did God actually say . . . ?" (Gen. 3:1).

The Serpent represented God as repressive and tyrannical: "You will not surely die. For God knows that when you eat of it your eyes will be opened, and you will be like God, knowing good and evil" (3:4–5). This was a devilishly clever half-truth in its appeal to the apparently irresistible aesthetic and intellectual desirability of the one forbidden fruit in the beautiful garden.

The first humans took the fruit, ate it and died—not at once in the physical sense, but that would eventually follow, for death is the unweaving of life. Life at its highest is a moral and spiritual relationship with God that is bound up with trust in and obedience to his word. So, according to an inexorable logic, death began with the disruption of that relationship. However, it did not end there. Aesthetic and physical death followed in due course, but death had begun its cruel tyranny, and the humans fled the presence of God. And, one might add, we have been running and hiding ever since.

Indeed, the topic of deception runs through the whole biblical storyline. In particular, it will form an important part of the story of Joseph, son of Jacob whose very name means "deceiver."

The biblical account of the way in which sin entered the world and brought disaster is not without its objectors. Indeed, many people not only refuse to take it seriously but also think that it presents a concept of God as repressive and anti-intellectual, determined to keep humans enslaved in naive and unworthy dependence. I wish to suggest that this is culpable misrepresentation arising through failure to read carefully exactly what the text of Genesis says.

Nowhere is this misrepresentation more publicly evident than in a fascinating piece of outdoor art on the campus of the University of California at San Diego. It is called *Snake Path* and was conceived and executed by well-known artist Alexis Smith. It forms part of the Stuart Collection, the website of which informs us that *Snake Path*

> consists of a winding 560-foot-long, 10-foot-wide footpath in the form of a serpent, whose individual scales are hexagonal pieces of colored slate, and whose head is inlaid in the approach to the Geisel Library. The tail wraps around an existing concrete pathway as a snake would wrap itself around a tree limb. Along the way, the serpent's slightly crowned body circles around a small "garden of Eden" with several fruit trees including a pomegranate. There is a marble bench with a quote from Thomas Gray: "Yet ah why should they know their fate / When sorrow never comes too late / And happiness too swiftly flies / Thought would destroy their Paradise / No more, where ignorance is bliss, tis folly to be wise." The path then passes a monumental granite book carved with a quote from Milton's *Paradise Lost*: "And wilt thou not be loath to leave this Paradise, but shalt possess a Paradise within thee, happier far."[5]

The website further explains:

> These pointed allusions to the biblical conflict between innocence and knowledge mark an apt symbolic path to the University's main repository of books. The concept of finding

---

5. Alexis Smith, *Snake Path*, 1992, UCSan Diego website, accessed September 6, 2018, http://stuartcollection.ucsd.edu/artist/smith-a.html.

sanctuary within oneself—outside the idealistic and protected confines of the university—speaks directly to the student on the verge of entering the "real world."[6]

However, the tree in the biblical account of the garden of Eden was not the tree of *knowledge*. It was the tree of the *knowledge of good and evil*, which is a completely different matter. The snake did not open up a path to the myriad kinds of knowledge that we associate with a university that could lead to human flourishing but only to one specific kind of knowledge—the knowledge of good and evil. That knowledge, gained by the first humans, was grim, dark, and painful and led to a rupture between them and God. That was not human flourishing; it was death in the making.

When the website claims that the *Snake Path* contains "pointed allusions to the biblical conflict between innocence and knowledge," the idea here seems to be that God holds people captive in a state of ignorance, withholding from them the knowledge that would lead to the realization of their full potential. This erroneous idea is the seedbed of much atheism. But it is a completely false reading of Genesis. Indeed, the idea that innocence was in the garden and knowledge outside it is the very opposite of the truth, as the biblical story makes very clear.

As we have seen, Genesis 2 describes how the garden was designed to be the place where the humans could develop their creative potential. The tragedy is that misreading this story has led to the perpetuation of the slander that God is the enemy of human flourishing rather than its author.

The Seed Project

To the Serpent that deceived the humans with that lie God says:

> I will put enmity between you and the woman,
> and between your offspring and her offspring;

---

6. Ibid.

he shall bruise your head,
and you shall bruise his heel. (Gen. 3:15)

It is a judgment, but it also forms the basis for an astonishing expectation for the future. By promising that the offspring of the woman is to triumph, God is declaring that humanity is not finished—far from it. The human story will be complex and full of frustration and difficulty; nevertheless, says God, a human will ultimately defeat the enemy.

This is not simply a prediction that God will triumph, an issue that was never in doubt. It is a prediction that humanity will triumph. In the end it will be the "seed of the woman," a human being, that will conquer the enemy.

Thus begins the story of the seed that, according to the New Testament, finds its ultimate focus in the One whom Paul calls the seed, or the offspring—that is, Jesus Christ (Gal. 3:16). Genesis contains the account of the initial trajectory of the seed. With the birth of Eve's first children, Cain and Abel, that trajectory begins. Far from life in that first family being harmonious and idyllic, the dire effects of the entry of sin into the world are revealed with devastating swiftness when Cain murders his brother Abel.

The life of the first human family is marred by fratricide in the first generation—a grim indicator of the difficulties that will lie in the path of eventually getting the seed into the world. Eve is left with one son—a murderer. But then she gives birth to another son, Seth, and with him the Seed Project regains its momentum: "To Seth also a son was born, and he called his name Enosh. At that time people began to call upon the name of the LORD" (Gen. 4:26).

Section 3: Judgment (Genesis 5:1–9:29)

The third major section of Genesis begins with the marker phrase in this form: "This is the book of the generations of Adam" (5:1). It then rapidly traces the offspring of Adam down to Noah. It chronicles increasing violence on the earth with some notable exceptions such as Enoch and Noah. The wickedness of humanity nevertheless reaches such a pitch that God decides to blot out human beings (6:6). At first sight this would seem to bring the Seed Project to a complete end. But there is a caveat in God's assessment: "But Noah found favor in the eyes of the LORD" (6:8). Accordingly, the text subsequently narrows its focus to the seed of Noah, noting this important transition by the use of the marker phrase once more (6:9). The rest of the section is dominated by the judgment of the flood through which Noah and his family are saved by the ark.

It is not our intention to discuss the flood narrative here except to point out that Jesus himself referred to it when discussing his return: "As were the days of Noah, so will be the coming of the Son of Man" (Matt. 24:37). Jesus uses the events surrounding the flood as a thought model to help his hearers understand something of the suddenness and unexpectedness of his future return "on the clouds of heaven with power and great glory" (v. 30).

The topic of judgment is understandably not very appealing to those who do not readily think of a final judgment as in any sense glorious. Yet this is a superficial reaction since the judgment of God is the obverse side of his love; in other words, a God who does not ultimately deal righteously with evil cannot be a God of love. Indeed, the fact that there is a final judgment tells us that our sense of right and wrong, our moral conscience, is not an illusion.

Contemporary atheists wax vitriolic whenever the judgment of God is mentioned. They claim to be interested in justice. Yet, according to them, the vast majority of human beings will never get justice for the simple reason that most do not get it in this life, and there is, according to them, no life after death in which there could be a final assessment. The terrorist or tyrant who murders his fellow human beings and eventually turns his gun upon himself escapes justice, according to atheism. This is deluded thinking, for we live in a moral universe, and God will see to it that justice will not only be done but will be seen to have been done. The famous

Marxist thinker Max Horkheimer, of the celebrated Frankfurt School, once said that he feared there might not be a God because, in that case, there would be no justice. He need not have feared on that account; this is a moral universe and God will see to it that justice will not only be done but will be seen to have been done.

To summarize: the first section of Genesis tells us that human beings are made in the image of God. The second section focuses on one important aspect of that image—that humans are moral beings. It then tells of the great deception that introduced sin into the world and gives intimations of how that damage will one day be undone as the seed of the woman triumphs. The third section points to the ultimate validation of that moral status in the judgment of God, a judgment tinged with mercy as Noah and his family are granted salvation.

Hence, another way of looking at the first part of Genesis is to see it as anticipating three major Christian doctrines: (1) creation; (2) sin and redemption; and (3) judgment and the last things.

2

The God of Abraham,
Isaac, and Jacob

We mentioned earlier that there are six major sections in Genesis. The final three sections are devoted to the family history of the patriarchs. After the familiar section marker, "These are the generations of . . . " (10:1), the fourth major section of the book initially moves swiftly down the generations as it outlines the beginnings of the great civilizations of the ancient Near East and their cities, such as Babel and Nineveh, that were to become famous as centers of great empires.

The active intervention of God at Babel to confuse the languages of the peoples is followed once again by a narrowing of the focus of the Seed Project to the descendants of Shem (11:10) and subsequently Terah and his son Abraham (11:27). Abraham was a towering figure that bestrides not only Genesis but also the whole biblical storyline. He was also Joseph's great-grandfather, and it is surely to be taken for granted that Joseph's early upbringing was filled with the exploits of Abraham. In order to understand Joseph's story, it will therefore be necessary to sketch in the stories that filled his childhood, memories of which may well have played a formative role in his life. At this point we shall trace the storyline briefly and only later add in detail as it becomes relevant.

Section 4: Abraham and His Sons (Genesis 10:1–25:11)

The account of Abraham's life starts when God makes a promise to him that has huge implications for the subsequent history of the world: "I will make of you a great nation . . . and in you all the families of the earth shall be blessed" (12:2–3). The remainder of the book, indeed of the Bible, tells us how that promise was and yet is to be fulfilled. However, within Genesis the first indicator of the scale of the blessing comes with Joseph, when the storyline widens out from the nomadic family of Abraham, his children, and grandchildren to Joseph, who is catapulted into a crucial position as governor of the empire of Egypt and in that capacity brings relief to a large part of the ancient world.

The promise of becoming a great nation naturally implied that Abraham and Sarah, his wife, would have children, and yet it soon became clear that, in their case, something had gone wrong with the physical processes involved in the transmission of life. They, like many other couples, seemed incapable of producing children. It is this circumstance that forms the initial focus of one of the major themes of the whole book: faith in God.

The Lord appeared to Abraham in a vision and spoke to him: "Fear not, Abram, I am your shield; your reward shall be very great" (15:1). Abraham's response showed his pain at being childless: "O Lord GOD, what will you give me, for I continue childless" (15:2). Abraham pointed out that because he had no natural heir, his servant Eliezer would become his legal heir, and the family would die out. Not so, said the Lord: "This man shall not be your heir; your very own son shall be your heir" (15:4). The Lord then bade Abraham count the stars and said: "So shall your offspring be" (15:5). Abraham's reaction was as brief as it was profound: "He believed the LORD, and he counted it to him as righteousness" (15:6).

With that statement we have reached the central theme of Genesis: trusting God and his word. There is a powerful logic here. The fatal wrong turn away from God consisted in putting trust in a voice other than God's—a constant danger for all of us in a world where we are bombarded with a multitude of voices all clamoring for our undivided attention. The way back to God must therefore be learning to listen to his voice and to trust what he says.

Abraham is held out to us in the biblical record as an outstanding example of what it means to trust what God has promised. As a result of his faith in God, Abraham was accounted righteous. That is, he was declared by God to be in a right relationship with him. In the language of the New Testament, he was justified by faith.

Abraham, though the most prominent, is not the first person in Genesis to trust God. The record of men and women of faith in Hebrews 11 includes Abel, Enoch, and Noah, who lived before Abraham. Nor is Abraham the last, for he is followed in that record by his wife, Sarah, then by his son Isaac, by Isaac's son Jacob, and finally (in Genesis, that is) by Jacob's son Joseph.

What is at once clear from the biblical record is that the Seed Project involves two things that operate simultaneously. There is the physical transmission of life through genetic processes with which we are all familiar. Children are born into the world without their permission. Each of us wakes up (so to speak) to find ourselves already here. That is the first process. The second element in the Seed Project is not a physical process at all. Nor is it automatic. It has to do with personal faith in God.

The New Testament captures this difference very well. According to John, faith is the essential prerequisite for the new birth. It is said of Jesus that "he came to his own, and his own people did not receive him. But to all who did receive him, who believed in his name, he gave the right to become children of God, who were born, not of blood nor of the will of the flesh nor of the will of man, but of God" (John 1:11–13).

The transmission of physical life depends on the decision of potential parents. Children cannot help being born physically; they have no say in the matter. It is completely different when it comes to the new birth. For it is not a physical process of that sort at all. Human beings are endowed by God, as we have seen from the second movement of Genesis, with the wonderful capacity of being able to form relationships. They can say yes or no; they can decide to put their trust in another or refrain from doing so. The key question for them is whether they are going to use this capacity to trust God. Thus, when Christ came into the world, some did not receive him. They freely refused to use their God-given ability to trust him. Others freely used that capacity to trust him and, because of that trust, they received eternal life as an unearned gift of God.

This matter of faith is central to Genesis and to the Bible as a whole, and it is therefore not surprising that it has been the subject of different kinds of misunderstanding that have led to confusion. For instance, some contend that if humans were capable of trusting God, it would mean that we contribute to our own salvation, thus contradicting the fact that salvation is by the grace of God and not by human merit. However, that is not the case.[1]

The apostle Paul heads off such confusion by going to great lengths to explain that faith is the very opposite of works, as a principle. He uses Abraham as an illustration of what is involved:

> What then shall we say was gained by Abraham, our forefather according to the flesh? For if Abraham was justified by works, he has something to boast about, but not before God. For what does the Scripture say? "Abraham believed God, and it was counted to him as righteousness." Now to the one who works, his wages are not counted as a gift but as his due. And to the one who does not work but believes in him who justifies the ungodly, his faith is counted as righteousness. (Rom. 4:1–5)

---

1. See my *Determined to Believe?: The Sovereignty of God, Freedom, Faith, and Human Responsibility* (Oxford, UK: Lion Hudson, 2017).

The statement "the one who does not work but believes" is a description of what Abraham did, and it shows that Paul understands that trusting is not working, even though the person trusting is exercising his own capacity to trust (note the emphasis on *his* faith).

Paul says the same thing in Ephesians 2:8–9: "For by grace you have been saved through faith. And this is not your own doing; it is the gift of God, not a result of works, so that no one may boast." Salvation is by grace; it is a magnificent gift of God, but it is appropriated by exercising the capacity to trust, which is another of God's great gifts to us, a gift that defines our very humanity as fashioned in God's image.

The way it all worked out in practice was far from smooth. Abraham trusted God, but nothing happened—at least not immediately. And into that unexplained vacuum came Sarah, his wife, suggesting an ancient form of surrogacy as a way to achieve the promised goal of having a child. She had an Egyptian maid who was probably one of the spoils of their embarrassing stay in Egypt when Sarah pretended to be Abraham's sister. Desperate for a child, Sarah presented Abraham with Hagar. It was thus that Ishmael was born. All went moderately well until, to Abraham and Sarah's great surprise, since they were old, Sarah herself gave birth to a son and named him Isaac. Unsurprisingly a tension arose between Sarah and Hagar that was only resolved when Hagar and Ishmael were sent away in a manner that raises many questions, although it is to be noticed that God spoke directly to the despairing Hagar and promised her that Ishmael would become a great nation (see Genesis 21).

Two more incidents in Isaac's life would have been stored in his grandson Joseph's memory. The first was when God told Abraham to take Isaac and sacrifice him on Mount Moriah. It was a morally puzzling and emotionally devastating request since all Abraham's hopes for significant posterity now rested in Isaac. And yet God had promised that there would be posterity, and so, as Paul tells us, Abraham reasoned that God would fulfill his promise even if he had to raise Isaac from the dead. However, just as Abraham was about to kill his son, God intervened and said, "Now I know that you fear God" (22:12) and pointed Abraham to a ram in the vicinity that he took and sacrificed instead of Isaac.

The second story is the romantic account of the way in which Abraham found a bride for Isaac. He sent his trusty servant back to the region of Haran from which he had originally come to seek a bride among Abraham's relatives. The servant prayed for guidance and at the watering hole encountered a beautiful young woman who fetched water for his camels and told him that she belonged to Abraham's wider family. Intense discussion followed, and the servant painted such a picture of Isaac, son of Abraham, that Rebekah was persuaded to leave her family and travel back with Abrahams's servant to marry a man she had never seen (see Genesis 24).

Not long afterward Abraham died (25:8), and with his death, section 4 of the book ends.

3

Isaac and His Sons

We now move to the account of the second generation, Isaac and his sons, Jacob and Esau.

Section 5: Isaac and His Sons (Genesis 25:12–35:29)

Since Jacob is to become the father of Joseph, in order to understand Joseph it is important that we get to know Jacob with a more detailed investigation. As in the account of Abraham, Jacob's birth story focuses on a woman who cannot bear children. Isaac took his wife Rebekah's distress to God in prayer, and she became pregnant with twins, one of which, Esau, was born just before his brother Jacob, whose tiny hand clasped Esau's heel—a circumstance that led to his name.

The name Jacob in Hebrew is taken from a word meaning "heel" or "rear" and is related to a verb meaning "to follow at the heel, assail, circumvent, or supplant," and to an adjective meaning "deceitful." The name, as we shall see, was extremely apposite.

The boys turned out to be as different as chalk and cheese. Esau was a man of the outdoors, a hunter, whereas Jacob preferred the quieter life of a shepherd. The parents had different favorites; Isaac favored Esau, and Rebekah, Jacob.

The first major milestone recorded about their adult lives occurs when Esau comes in one day exhausted from hunting and sees that Jacob has brewed up some very appetizing stew. He asks for some, and Jacob, showing the wily streak that was so to characterize him, says that Esau can have the food provided he gives up his birthright as the firstborn son in the family. Esau agrees so readily that it is obvious that an abstract concept such as a birthright, which relates to a distant future, has no interest for him. A full stomach now—that's the real thing.

This incident was to haunt them both for years, compounded, as it was, by what happened when Isaac was old, blind, and ready to die. Isaac asked Esau to go hunting and prepare a game stew for him, after which he would bless him as the firstborn before dying. Rebekah, on hearing this, told Jacob to get a goat that she would prepare in the style of game. She next dressed Jacob in the skin of the goat to give his arms the kind of roughness that Esau's had and then she sent Jacob in with the food and told him to pretend to be Esau and steal the blessing due to his brother. Isaac could not see Jacob, and he was initially hesitant because he thought that the voice was Jacob's, but in the end he decided to be guided by smell and touch. He was deceived by the conflicting signals coming from his senses, and gave Esau's blessing to Jacob, thinking that Jacob was Esau. Jacob made a speedy exit just before his brother returned with his game stew. Not surprisingly Esau was very angry, bitterly disappointed, and disgusted to hear what had happened. Jacob's tiny hand now grown large had grasped the blessing due to his brother by deceiving his father. He was behaving true to his name—the deceiver or supplanter.

This trait in Jacob is found to a certain extent at least in every human heart, and it represents a major theme in all that is yet to come in Genesis.

Rebekah, seeing Esau's fury and hatred for his brother, subtly persuades Isaac to let Jacob go to his uncle Laban in the hope of finding a wife there from their kin, just as Isaac had done years before.

It was a very long journey, around 550 miles in total, that took him up via Damascus and Carchemish to Haran in Mesopotamia. Not long after he set out, Jacob dreamed his famous dream of a ladder extending up to heaven from the stone that served as his pillow. In his vision Jacob observed some angels ascending on the ladder to the top and others descending again. When he saw this, he said, "Surely the LORD is in this place. . . . This is none other than the house of God, and this is the gate of heaven" (28:16–17). Jacob regarded this encounter with God as so significant that he gave a name to the place where it occurred, Bethel, meaning "the house of God."

Doubtless Jacob was familiar with God, the Almighty, who dwelt in heaven, but at Bethel Jacob discovered something remarkable and new about God. The vision led him to exclaim: "Surely the LORD is in *this* place"; that is, God was right beside him—not at the top of the ladder in heaven but at the bottom of the ladder, right where Jacob was resting. God was, so to speak, running the universe from where Jacob was.

The remaining imagery supports this idea, for the gate of an ancient city was not simply its entrance; it was the place where the local government officials sat and held their meetings to manage the affairs of the city. For instance, Lot sat in the gate of Sodom; that is, he was an official in the local administration. The gate of heaven, then, was the place from which God's angelic ministers received their orders, carried them out, and returned for more. In other words, Jacob found himself at God's administrative center. In this kind of context the term "house of God" is likely to carry the connotation, not so much of God's dwelling, but of God's government. Just as in the UK, when we speak of the House of Windsor we don't mean the palace in which our queen resides; we mean her government, her reigning house.

God speaks to Jacob and, impressing upon him his nearness and his willingness to be with the man, he promises to guide him into his future. Jacob, ever out for a deal, tries to bargain with God: if God will do this, that, and the other for him, then God will be Jacob's God. It seems a pretty inadequate response, possibly hinting at a desire deep within Jacob to keep God at arm's length, perhaps to give himself more wriggle room. As we know only too well, the human heart is like that. Even when God appears and offers his guidance and direction, and we know it is real, there may linger that deceitful, essentially devilish idea that God will cramp our style in some way.

In the years to come Jacob would have to learn, often the hard way, that God was overwhelmingly for him. God would direct him and yet treat him with dignity as a responsible human being. God would educate him as to the nature of his rule, and some of that education would be painful. Jacob was to be the leader of a nation with a unique role in the world. As we now follow him and his family, we shall find ample evidence of the complexity of his relationship with the Lord.

Jacob Leaves His Home and Goes to Laban

Jacob continued his lengthy journey until he found himself at a well where he met his uncle Laban's beautiful daughter Rachel. The encounter was very like that of grandfather Abraham's servant who found Rebekah as a wife for Abraham's son Isaac. Rebekah eventually became Jacob's mother.

Jacob, who must have seen it as a providential event, fell in love with Rachel, and he hastened to do a deal with Laban: he would work for Laban for seven years to gain Rachel as wife. However, on the wedding morning, to his surprise and horror, he found not Rachel but her older sister, Leah, in his tent. Jacob was furious and accused Laban of cheating him. Laban countered by saying that it was not the custom of their tribe to give the younger daughter in marriage before the elder.

Jacob's deceiving character had caught up with him. Years earlier, Jacob, the younger son, had pretended to be his older brother

Esau to deceive his father Isaac—the younger had gone before the older. Not only that, but Leah did not (or so it is assumed) possess Rachel's beauty. Jacob was now getting to know by painful experience what it was like to be deceived, in one sense a real taste of his own medicine that he had meted out to his father. Longfellow's poem captures it exactly:

> Though the mills of God grind slowly,
> Yet they grind exceeding small;
> Though with patience He stands waiting,
> With exactness grinds He all.[1]

Genesis is silent as to the details of Jacob's reaction, but it is not hard to imagine that the lesson was not lost on him. This was the government of God at work. God treats Jacob as fully responsible for his behavior to his father and brother, but now God sees to it that circumstances combine to force Jacob to experience the very same sort of behavior.

How complex this is we can see from the fact that it happened to be the local custom in those parts not to give the younger preference over the older. That tradition had probably been around for centuries, yet we are invited to see the hand of God behind it. Indeed, in Paul's major discussion in Romans 9–11 of the relationship between God's sovereignty and human responsibility, he uses Jacob and Esau as examples of the intricacy of God's dealings.

Laban would have to face lessons about deception and trickery when he in turn was deceived by Jacob (and, indeed, by Rachel), but at this point there was a further bitter lesson for Jacob. Isaac had failed to distinguish between Jacob and Esau because of his weak vision. Presumably, there was plenty of light; the problem was with Isaac's eyes. Presumably, also, there was nothing wrong with Jacob's eyes as he went into the marital tent on his wedding night, but he failed to tell the difference between Leah and Rachel

1. Henry Wadsworth Longfellow, "Mills of God," *Oxford Dictionary of Proverbs*, ed. J. Speake (Oxford, UK: Oxford University Press, 2015), 208.

because there was no light; in the dark people look (and, we might add in these circumstances, feel) essentially the same; there is no mention of voice, so we must presume that both Leah and Jacob were silent that night. Jacob, like his father, Isaac, before him, had to learn the dangers of trusting his physical senses when trying to determine someone's identity.

We might well ask about the principle here. What does the story tell us of Jacob's views of women and marriage? All we are told is that Rachel was "beautiful in form and appearance" (Gen. 29:17), a description that we will find used of Joseph in the context of his attempted seduction by Potiphar's wife. Rachel's beauty seems to have had an instant rapturous effect on Jacob when he met her.

Physical attraction follows the eye, an organ in which the story takes great interest. Rachel's older sister Leah is said to have had "weak" or "soft" eyes (29:17). This lack of detail leaves us comparing Rachel's good looks with Leah's eyes. Some imagine that Leah was weak-eyed in the physical sense, such that her features were spoiled, but what if that were not the case so much as that she had eyes that drew attention to themselves because they were mirrors to a tender soul?

Could it be that what is hinted at here is the difference between the inner and the outer person, depth of soul as opposed to superficial glamour? In the end Jacob went for the glamour. Not that desire for and responsiveness to beauty were wrong, but it is noteworthy that the text is silent on the important question as to whether Rachel was suitable as a wife for Jacob.

Cunning Laban saw that Jacob's heart was set on Rachel, and he leveraged this fact to make a further business deal that exploited the situation—and Jacob. The deal was that Jacob could wed Rachel as well straight after the week of wedding festivities for his marriage to Leah had run its course, but for that privilege, he would have to work for seven further years without pay, effectively as a servant in his father-in-law's house. It was a strange arrangement in a culture where the bride's father usually had to come up with a hefty dowry in order to get a good husband for his daughter. Laban exploited Jacob's passion for Rachel to the full and got him to work for that which he should normally have been given.

We know very little about the relationships between the sisters or about Laban's family, although there is a great deal of speculation on the part of Jewish commentators as to whether, for example, Rachel, not wishing to humble her sister by marrying first, actually went along with the deception and even, some think, helped it to succeed. Nor do we know what part, if any, Leah played in the deceiving of Jacob, though it is difficult to think that she had no idea what was going on! However, we just don't know, and I conclude that the text concentrates on the things we do need to know so that we should be content with looking at them.

Jacob's Family Life

Bigamy was never an ideal way to start married life as it inevitably led to favoritism and intense rivalry. Jacob had been his mother's favorite, and now he was starting married life with strong prejudice in his heart against one of his wives. It was a very unhappy situation for Leah. Just try to imagine it. This is, after all, supposed to be the story of a family for whom God cares.

Well, then, what about Leah? Doesn't God care for her and, what is more, the many, many women who share her situation? Here she was, through no fault of her own, perhaps genetically endowed with facial features that were not attractive to men, married, as a result of a process in which she was not involved, to a man who clearly did not love her but had to put up with her because of certain customs of the local tribe. A victim of circumstances beyond her control, she was trapped in a loveless marriage.

Her story is for many a microcosm of the human condition in which they find themselves: the feeling that life has been unfair from the start; the envy of others who are better endowed physically or mentally; belonging to a family in which a sibling is ostentatiously favored; being a victim of circumstances that seem to have combined to fill life with cruel twists; the tears produced by rejection or bitter taunting. The list is endless.

And who of us is exempt—either from being a victim or, indeed, being a victimizer? And God, if there is a God, is surely only interested in the strong and handsome, in those who thrive and flourish, who are popular and wealthy and fit? He doesn't even see me, and if he did, he wouldn't be interested, would he?

But God did see Leah. He saw that she was hated, and he did something about it: "He opened her womb, but Rachel was barren" (29:31). This marks the beginning of the saga of the family into which Joseph will be born. Leah's first son was called Reuben, a name that means "see a son" and was chosen to express her deep feelings, as she herself explained: "The LORD has looked upon my affliction; for now my husband will love me" (29:32). This is quite remarkable since Leah was raised in a pagan home, as we may deduce from the fact that when Jacob eventually takes his family away from Laban, Rachel steals his household gods.

Yet, along the way, so far, Leah appears to have come not only to believe in the God of Jacob but personally to trust him with the heartbreaks in her daily life.

One can imagine that during the seven years when Jacob was in the home working to earn the right to marry Rachel, he regaled the family with the stories of his father and grandfather. And uncle Laban likely recalled the way that Isaac's servant turned up at his (Laban's) father's home and asked on Isaac's behalf for the hand of Laban's sister Rebekah in marriage. No doubt Jacob took the opportunity to recite the marvelous similarity between that occasion and his own arrival at Uncle Laban's home. There would have been talk about God, the lessons of faith that Abraham and Sarah had had to learn about the ways of God and his guidance and protection of their lives.

All of this may well have made a deep impression on Leah so that somewhere during that time, she came to trust in the God of Abraham, even though it is likely that the attitude of the one who had brought her the message—Jacob—may well have been thoughtless and even cruel at times toward her. It was clear to Leah's tender eyes that Jacob had eyes only for Rachel, and that must have been very hard to take.

Yet Leah had somehow been able to distinguish between the messenger and the message—a feat that many people today, with vastly more knowledge, seem incapable of doing. They claim that they are not interested in God because "there are so many hypocrites in the church" or someone claiming to be a Christian was angry with them (possibly justifiably!), etc. Many such people, however, have never taken the time to read or listen to the storyline of the Bible. Such experiences are rather superficial.

But they are not the only kind. No family is free of tension, of petty jealousies, white lies, favoritisms, and rivalries, to say nothing of darker things, and when these are mixed up with professing Christianity, the combination can be disastrous. What, for example, is a child to think of God when he is abused by an adult who outwardly professes Christianity, or when she is witness to constant angry outbursts and even violence between churchgoing parents, or when he sees his father abandoning his mother for some younger woman in his office?

Leah had heard the story and grasped enough of the message to become a child of Abraham by trusting the God of Abraham. Her faith in God had grown in spite of Jacob's behavior, and the worse the family tensions became, the more she took them to God—at least, initially. Hence the name of her first child expresses her belief that the Lord has seen her loveless predicament.

And it is she who chooses the child's name. That seems quite unusual in an ancient patriarchal culture. After all, in this particular family line Abraham gave the name Isaac to his son, and Jacob received his name from both his parents; yet now it is the mother, Leah, who names her son. Or at least this is all that the text says, for it is hard to imagine that the name was given without Jacob's approval. However, if so, they must have discussed the choice of name, and that may well have given Leah the opportunity to come into the open about her fears and concerns regarding Jacob's attitude toward her.

Another son Simeon (meaning "heard") soon followed, and, once more, the name reflected the ongoing pain in Leah's heart: "Because the LORD has heard that I am hated, he has given me this son also" (29:33).

A third son was called Levi ("joined"), and she said: "Now this time my husband will be attached to me, because I have borne him three sons" (29:34).

It is not hard to see that her children's names were deliberately chosen not only to form a record of her own personal emotional and spiritual journey but to be a constant reminder to Jacob that his attitude to his wife and the mother of his children—and to God—was far from what it should be. Can you imagine Jacob having to explain to someone how his children got their names?

This is not the first time in Genesis that names have been chosen in this way to reflect an experience of God. Think of Hagar, who, like Leah, was despised. When Hagar was cast out of the home, God appeared to her in the desert and made promises to her regarding how her son Ishmael would become a great nation. Ishmael means "God hears," and the name performed the same function for Hagar as the name Simeon ("heard") did for Leah. Not only that but Hagar gave a name to God: "a God of seeing" (16:13). Reuben means "see a son," as noted earlier. The similarity between the experiences and the names is quite remarkable.

God had fulfilled Leah's desire for children, and she would therefore be highly regarded as a mother in her ancient society. Yet, unsurprisingly, she wanted more; she longed for her husband's affection and love.

But in spite of producing three sons for Jacob, it appears that he did not grow any closer to Leah as a person. He treated her as a means (of child production) and not as an end (a person to be valued in her own right). This, humanly speaking, is one of the hardest things to bear, and many in our societies have to bear it.

When Leah's fourth son was born she called him Judah and said: "This time I will praise the LORD" (29:35). Something had changed in Leah's heart. Gone was any expectation of an improved relationship between her and Jacob; she seems to have accepted that it just wouldn't happen. Leah shows no obvious trace of bitterness. Indeed, all she wished to do was praise the Lord and celebrate that fact in the name of her fourth son. She appears, therefore, to have found deep strength of character and resolve to rise above her circumstances and their unfairness.

She had every reason to be consumed with bitterness and disappointment. It was not her fault that she did not possess Rachel's glamorous looks. Nor was it her fault that she was trapped in a loveless relationship with Jacob. And yet she seems to have gotten over it; at least, she had not let it get to her. Her faith in God helped her triumph in spite of the fact that Jacob was scarcely a role model of a believing husband. Noticeably, as far as the text is concerned, Leah speaks more about God than Jacob does.

There was something even bigger happening at the time. What Leah did not know—indeed, what she could not know—was that as she named the children, she was choosing the names that will one day adorn the gates of God's eternal city, according to the vision given to John in the book of Revelation (see Rev. 21:12). The very entrances to that city promised to Abraham will bear the names of her sons.

One cannot help thinking that in the story of Leah and her children, we get a glimpse behind the scenes as to the deep love of God that not only understands but can and eventually will compensate for the pain and disappointment that his people experience on earth. God had purposes for Leah's children that went far beyond anything that she could have imagined at the time, and she probably first learned about them when she reached her heavenly home.

We need to pause and think about the implications of Leah's story. Some might think that in the grand scale of things, the heartaches of a young woman like Leah are of no real importance. This is just what life is like—tough and hard for most; easy for very few. But that would be to miss something of immense importance: God's interest and concern for the minutest detail of our everyday, even humdrum, lives that can make our experiences of eternal significance. We can experience heartache, pain, disappointment, and even disillusionment as we fight our way to the realization that God does hear and God does see, but arriving at that realization does not guarantee an easy resolution of our problems. In the midst of it all, our confidence in God is stretched by being encouraged to praise him independently of our circumstances—not fatalistically, but in genuine acceptance and trust in his presence and support.

Many years ago I told this story of Leah to a conference of students. During my talk, I noticed a young woman in the audience who had a beautiful face—at least, one half of it was beautiful, but the other was disfigured by a very large birthmark. When I had finished, she immediately stood up and came to the front of the auditorium and lifted her face to the audience. Then she said something like this: "For the first time in my life I wish today to say something about my trust in God. Listening to this beautiful story of Leah has helped me to get to a place where, without any sense of fatalism, I can accept the way that I am and trust the Lord for the ability to cope with the consequences." There wasn't a dry eye in the place, and I found myself wondering whether I had come that far in my trust in the Lord.

Meanwhile, Rachel was smoldering with jealousy. In contrast with Leah, she enjoyed all Jacob's love and attention, yet she did not have what Leah had—children. Her good looks and attentive husband did not compensate for the lack of a family. So in her desperation for children of her own, she demanded them from Jacob, who became angry with her. She offered him her maid as a surrogate and in that way gained two sons, Dan and Naphtali. Not to be outdone, Leah resorted to the same tactic, offering her maid to Jacob, and as a result Gad and Asher were born. This sibling rivalry escalated when Reuben brought to Leah, his mother, some mandrake roots, regarded at the time as aphrodisiacs. Rachel bargained with Leah: Leah could sleep with Jacob that night provided Rachel had the mandrakes. Leah faced Jacob with her "deal," he did what she requested, and Issachar was born. Then Leah herself had another son, Zebulun, followed by Dinah, the only daughter in the family that we know of.

Finally, we are explicitly told that God intervened and opened Rachel's womb, mandrakes or no mandrakes, and she bore her own firstborn son, Joseph. His name, meaning "may he add," reflects her desire for further sons. She would eventually have one more son, Benjamin, who will also play a prominent role in Joseph's life.

4

Jacob and Family Return to the Promised Land; Meeting God and Esau

After Jacob's favorite wife had given birth to a son, Jacob, not surprisingly, wished to get away from under Laban's feet and set up an independent family. After some very crafty and slippery dealings that may well have lasted several years, Jacob eventually gathered his family and flocks, and without informing Laban, he set out to return to his father Isaac in Canaan.

When Laban finds out, he is furious. After all, Jacob has been a major income generator for him. So Laban set out in pursuit. God intervened and warned Laban to be very careful and "not to say anything to Jacob, either good or bad" (Gen. 31:24).

Joseph may well have been old enough, though still a child, to later recall the tense meeting between his father and Laban, which resulted in a lot of straight talk. Eventually Jacob and Laban came to an agreement and sealed it by setting up a heap of stones as a witness. They had a final meal together and went their separate ways. The separation was final. Jacob was free of Laban.

However, Jacob realized that there was someone else he must face—Esau, the brother he had cheated years before. So far as we know, there had been no contact between the brothers for a long time. Anticipating an uncomfortable confrontation, to say the least, Jacob sent out messengers who confirmed his worst fears: Esau was coming to meet him with an army of four hundred men. Jacob was terrified and divided his people and flocks into two groups in the hope that one of them would escape if Esau attacked.

He then prayed, an activity that seems not to have been one of his major priorities. In his prayer he reminded God that God himself had told him to go back to his kindred. He expressed himself as unworthy of all the love and faithfulness he had been shown, and he pleaded with the Lord to deliver him from the hand of his brother Esau.

Jacob's sense of guilt made him nervous, and in the hope of softening Esau's mood, he sent gifts of livestock ahead of him in two waves. Perhaps Jacob felt this was a way of recompensing Esau for the theft of the birthright years before.

Finally, at night, Jacob took his two wives, his two female servants, his eleven children, and his servants and possessions and helped them ford the river Jabbok. We don't know if Jacob discussed the situation with his family, but certainly they were aware of Jacob's mounting tension.

Jacob lingered behind and, alone in the darkness, no doubt with increasing trepidation, imagined that the next person he'd encounter will be Esau. He had presumably decided, maybe to protect his family, that he must face Esau alone. Yet he was not alone. For without warning, in the middle of the night, he found himself under surprise attack, and before he could realize what was happening, he became involved in a deadly wrestling match with a man. He probably thought at first that it was his brother Esau who had failed to be mollified by the gifts and had now come to fight him. His future will be decided by hand-to-hand combat in the night.

It is hard to imagine what thoughts crowded Jacob's mind: guilt at how he had treated Esau, and failure to patch things up; the futility of his life if he did not survive; the awful predicament of his family. Yet as the wrestling progressed, it slowly dawned on Jacob that there was something very strange about the encounter.

Wrestling? Is that what he would expect Esau to do? Well, obviously not if the intent were to kill Jacob. That would be much more effectively done with a club, knife, sword, or bow. You don't wrestle someone to kill him, although wrestling can lead to death, usually by accident rather than design. You wrestle someone to prove that you are top dog, the strongest stag in the rut, the most powerful bison in the herd, by demonstrating that your body is stronger and that you can out-think the other's tactics and bring him to submit. You wish him to remain very much alive, acknowledging your power over him.

And Jacob had been a wrestler all his life, not so much physically, as far as we know, since Esau was the more physical and outdoorsy of the two. Jacob was a clever psychological schemer, wrestling people into giving him what he wanted and making them think, at least for long enough, that they wanted it too. There is something more about wrestling: it is close combat. You get involved with your opponent at close range. You put pressure on him, and he puts pressure on you. You can't get away from him to attack at a distance. It saps your physical and mental energy, and it can be very painful.

Nowhere is this more evident than in family life—then and now. Jacob had wrestled with his father, mother, brother, uncle, and wives (and watched them wrestle with one another), and he had outwitted them all, or so he imagined.

No, this strange opponent was not Esau. It was someone altogether different, and yet so evenly matched with Jacob that Jacob may well have begun to think he could win. Then his opponent suddenly put out his hand and touched Jacob's hip joint, which at once dislocated and brought the fight to an end.

You cannot wrestle if you have a dislocated joint, especially the massive swivel that is the hip joint. Yet Jacob, who must have been convinced by now that there was a divine dimension in what was happening, did the only thing he could think of. Using his arms, which were still strong, he clung on to the man for grim death—clinging like he did in Rebekah's womb to Esau's heel. The victor said, "Let me go, for the day has broken." But Jacob replied: "I will not let you go unless you bless me" (32:26).

Jacob's opponent asked, "What is your name?" (32:27).

We cannot help thinking back to the time when Jacob's almost blind father Isaac had asked him the same question, and Jacob had lied. "I am Esau," he had said. He had lied to gain his father's blessing. But now, in this close encounter with God, lying was no longer possible. He would get no blessing from God that way. He had to admit who he was—the scheming, manipulating, supplanting, heel-grasping Jacob. He had spent his life manipulating others. He now had to learn that he could not do the same with God. He had to face it; if he was to get God's blessing, the old Jacob had to go. And so it was. The next thing the victorious wrestler said was, "Your name shall no longer be called Jacob, but Israel, for you have striven with God and with men, and have prevailed" (32:28).

Jacob then asked for his conqueror's name and was told that the question was inappropriate: "Why is it that you ask my name?" (32:29). The stranger could ask Jacob for his name, but Jacob was not permitted to ask him.

Through his pain and exhaustion Jacob realized that something unique had happened—he had met God. Accordingly, he called the place of his encounter Peniel, a name that means "the face of God." He said, "For I have seen God face to face, and yet my life has been delivered" (32:30).

What does the name "Israel" really mean? We can think of several ways in which Jacob had struggled with both men and God, but in what sense had Jacob prevailed? He certainly had not prevailed physically with his assailant, but he had prevailed in hanging on until he received God's blessing. Did his new name carry the idea that Jacob was now a prince with God, or did it mean that God ruled over Jacob? Scholars hint at ambiguities here, and they may well be deliberate in order to communicate the idea that the man who is a prince with God is the man who has learned the rule of God in his own life.

What is clear, in any event, is that the change of Jacob's name to Israel left a permanent mark, not only on his character but also on his body, for he limped for the rest of his life. He could never wrestle effectively again. He had become a wiser man, aware as never before of his vulnerability.

The night before Peniel he'd been expecting to see Esau, and the prospect made him fearful and distressed. What actually happened, though, was unique in all of his experience and, indeed, in the whole biblical storyline. It was to make him the head of a nation, the nation of Israel. Its members would be called his children, the children of Israel. And these children were constantly to recall the wrestling of Jacob at Peniel by refraining from eating meat from around the hip joint of an animal. That means, of course, that the incident was open for public discussion, and we can well imagine that Jacob's family were eager to hear from him what he had learned from it.

Thinking about this story prompts the question: What relevance has this to anyone today? One thing is obvious: most if not all of us, Christian or not, are wrestling with something, are we not? But we usually call it "struggling." We are struggling with ourselves, our circumstances, our health, or with other people in all sorts of ways that, if we are honest, take up a great deal of our time and energy.

Some of our struggles are what we might call "negative"; they are not doing us any good. What shall I gain if I win this or that particular battle, put one over on this or that particular person, or scheme my way into wrangling a higher salary or recognition than I am entitled to, or gain promotion by subtly and untraceably putting down others? What will my reputation look like if I "prevail" in any of the multitudinous scenarios that we can so easily—oh, so very easily—imagine?

We struggle with family life—parental favoritism, sibling rivalry, hurt, perceived unfairness in legacy distribution, and a host of other things.

We struggle internally—with fear, uncertainty, low self-esteem, anger, guilt, envy, jealousy, pride, and desire, to name but a few of the obvious sources.

Other struggles are positive—the struggle to maintain our witness to God, to develop a stronger Christian character, to become kinder, fairer, more loving, or more attentive, or to listen rather than talk.

Just stop for a moment and think or, better still, write down all the issues that you are struggling with today. Look at them all and then listen to God's question to Jacob: "What is your name?"

The question of personal identity is not an easy question to answer. Yet perhaps the story of Peniel offers real hope as it tells of a God who gave Jacob a completely new name that transcended all his struggles and redefined him. It is not that there was none of the old Jacob left, as we shall eventually see, but there was something new in him that was not there before.

Jacob's story is an Old Testament story, so we must not expect to be able to draw straight lines from it to the New Testament. However, certain elements of the story remind us of similar things in the New Testament. One example is name change. Through their encounters with Christ, Simon became Peter, and Saul became Paul. More generally, the risen Lord has promised to give a new name to those who "overcome" or "conquer" in the struggle to hold fast their witness to him (Rev. 2:17).

Lying behind this is the wonderful fact that those who trust Christ as Savior and Lord are given a new life; they are born again by the Holy Spirit, who now indwells them and gives them new powers to cope with the struggles of everyday life. We are told:

> Likewise the Spirit helps us in our weakness. For we do not know what to pray for as we ought, but the Spirit himself intercedes for us with groanings to deep for words. . . . And we know that for those who love God all things work together for good, for those who are called according to his purpose. (Rom. 8:26, 28)

There is more. The overwhelming effect of Peniel on Jacob was that, in some sense, he had seen God face-to-face. Now Scripture tells us that, strictly speaking: "No one has ever seen God; the only God, who is at the Father's side, he has made him known" (John 1:18). We may surely deduce from this statement that whenever men or women are said to have seen God, what is actually involved is that God the Son has revealed him. We call such events "theophanies" or "Christophanies."

A New Testament example that parallels Peniel in some way is the transfiguration of Jesus. Its importance is shown by the fact that we have three accounts of it in the Gospels and one in 2 Peter. Although within the incident itself there is no element of wrestling with God, its immediate context is a real struggle in the lives of Jesus's disciples, especially Peter. Not only that but the narrative starts with Jesus asking the disciples about his identity: "'But who do you say that I am?' Simon Peter replied, 'You are the Christ, the Son of the living God'" (Matt. 16:15–16).

Not long after this Jesus announced that he must go to Jerusalem where he would suffer, be killed, and rise the third day. The disciples were devastated, particularly Peter who began to rebuke him: "Far be it from you, Lord!" (Matt. 16:22). In other words, "No way!" Peter had, by this time, invested nearly three years of his time, energy, and resources on Jesus and his mission. He thought that all this was going to be wasted; he was going to lose it all.

Jesus replied to the effect that if Peter, and anyone else, wished to save his life, he would have to be prepared to lose it for Christ's sake. He made the famous statement: "For what will it profit a man if he gains the whole world and forfeits his soul? Or what shall a man give in exchange for his soul? For the Son of Man is going to come with his angels in the glory of his Father, and then he will repay each person according to what he has done" (Matt. 16:26–27).

Peter thought he was losing his life, that is, in the sense of what made life *life* for him. If Jesus was going to be rejected, suffer, and die, then Peter was surely on the losing side. It was all very confusing, and Peter struggled to understand it. And, in any case, how could he or anyone else know that all Jesus said was true?

But Jesus was not finished. "Truly, I say to you, there are some standing here who will not taste death until they see the Son of Man coming in his kingdom" (Matt. 16:28).

He was going to answer Peter's internal struggle by giving him (and two others, James and John) powerful evidence that he, Jesus, would one day gloriously return. They were going to see something very special that would convince them of this, something very like Jacob's experience at Peniel. The crucial point in Jesus's statement is that seeing the kingdom of God would be a before-death experience. For it is surely obvious that if Jesus is who he claims to be, then death will instantly remove all uncertainty. A nanosecond after death everyone will know that the kingdom of God is real. The important thing, therefore, is, how can we be convinced that it is real before we die?

Less than a week later, Jesus took the three disciples up on a high mountain, and "he was transfigured before them, and his face shone like the sun, and his clothes became white as light" (Matt. 17:2). Years later Peter reflected on what happened:

> For we did not follow cleverly devised myths when we made known to you the power and coming of our Lord Jesus Christ, but we were eyewitnesses of his majesty. For when he received

honor and glory from God the Father, and the voice was borne
to him by the Majestic Glory, "This is my beloved Son, with
whom I am well pleased," we ourselves heard this very voice
borne from heaven, for we were with him on the holy mountain. (2 Pet. 1:16–18)

This was surely Peter's Peniel. It was an experience of seeing the
glory of God that banished forever any doubts that there was an
eternal realm, that the kingdom of God was real, and that Jesus
would one day return.

We might well say, "But I was not at Peniel or on the mountain of transfiguration. What about me?" Peter was aware of this
and indicates another way in which the Lord reveals himself to
believers:

And we have the prophetic word more fully confirmed, to which
you will do well to pay attention as to a lamp shining in a dark
place, until the day dawns and the morning star rises in your
hearts, knowing this first of all, that no prophecy of Scripture
comes from someone's own interpretation. For no prophecy was
ever produced by the will of man, but men spoke from God as
they were carried along by the Holy Spirit. (2 Pet. 1:19–21)

In other words, Scripture can have the same effect for us as the
transfiguration (or Peniel) had for those involved. Scripture has
a supernatural dimension, which is why when we read it as it describes Peniel or the transfiguration, God can speak through it to
make it real in our lives today.

Such encounters with God are very special and do not occur
all the time. But long ago Jesus promised to reveal himself to his
disciples by the Holy Spirit, and that promise is as valid today
as it was when he said it (John 15:26–27). We are encouraged to
count on it.

Jacob limped away from Peniel and forever after. The limp reminded him that he was not, after all, a self-sufficient man living

in the fast lane. The limp slowed him down and humbled him as he recognized his human limitations and frailty. Yes, he had had an exalted experience of God, but this treasure, he now saw, was contained in a very brittle earthen vessel. It was only by relying on God's grace and power that he could make his way in life.

In that vulnerable condition he had to face his estranged brother Esau. The very next thing he saw as dawn broke after his encounter with God was Esau in the distance bearing down upon him with a substantial private army of four hundred men, about which Jacob had been informed by his servants a few days before.

Jacob then arranged his family in groups: his two female servants with their (Jacob's) children in front, then Leah and her own children, and finally Rachel and Joseph last. One wonders what Joseph was thinking as he watched his dad limp (where had he got the limp?) past them all and slowly advance toward Esau, pausing seven times to bow to the ground, obviously fearing the worst.

One wonders even more how it all appeared to Esau when he saw his brother who had cheated him limping toward him, demonstrating his vulnerability and bowing in submission to show repentance and contrition.

Esau, an emotional and impulsive man, as we know, was immediately overwhelmed by something he never expected and, overcome by emotion, he "ran to meet him and embraced him and fell on his neck and kissed him, and they wept" (Gen. 33:4).

The night before, Jacob had found himself with arms locked around a man who might well have been Esau. He now actually had his arms around Esau but not to wrestle. In their clinging together were mingled repentance, forgiveness, and reconciliation—a cathartic moment of immense significance. Jacob had no time to plead with Esau with whatever words he had planned to say. He was overwhelmed by Esau's action.

As young Joseph watched this remarkable sight, he had no idea that he and his brothers would eventually have to face the very same issues of repentance, forgiveness, and reconciliation. Joseph would have learned from this, however, that reconciliation is possible even in the most unpromising situations.

And as we look on, we are instinctively reminded of our Lord's parable of the prodigal, or lost son, which has to do with a father of two sons and matters of inheritance. In that story, as the repentant delinquent returned, "his father saw him and felt compassion, and ran and embraced him and kissed him" (Luke 15:20). The man had insisted on his inheritance even before his father died and had then wasted all the resources his father had blessed him with. The father, seeing his son's repentant attitude, forgave him and warmly received him back. His brother, piqued at what he regarded as an obscenely extravagant gesture of forgiveness, refused point-blank to join in the festivities.

It was Jacob's burning desire to get his father's blessing with all it implied for inheritance that had led to the rift with Esau at the beginning. And having gotten it by underhanded means, Jacob had been forced to depart and go to a far country where, unlike the prodigal, he had become rich and not poor. Now Jacob was coming back home and had to meet Esau, his elder brother, whom he might well have expected to behave like the elder brother in Jesus's parable had he known about it. Yet it was Esau who, in his unexpected magnanimous attitude to Jacob, showed the heart of the father in the parable.

As the intense emotion of the moment of reconciliation passed, Esau noticed the groups of women and children standing nearby and asked who they were. Jacob introduced them as "the children whom God has graciously given your servant" (Gen. 33:5). He doesn't mention his wives, possibly to avoid reminding Esau of the tension in their parental home over the matter of who Esau and Jacob would marry, and also the fact that seeking a bride was the excuse to get Jacob away from home and from Esau so that Esau could not harm him. Following Jacob's example, his wives and children deferentially prostrated themselves before Esau.

Esau then asks about the droves of livestock that had been sent to him, and Jacob tells him honestly that they were intended to gain his favor. In the manner of the East, Esau refuses the gift at first until Jacob insists, indeed strongly insists: "No, please, if I have found favor in your sight, then accept my present from my hand. For I have seen your face, which is like seeing the face of God, and you have accepted me" (33:10).

The night before, Jacob had seen God face-to-face. Now he says to his brother that he was seeing his face like the face of God. Of course Esau knew nothing of Jacob's encounter, yet the use of the expression "face of God" by Jacob here seems to indicate that there was an important connection in Jacob's mind. Could it be that Jacob was beginning to grasp that his brother, in common with all human beings, had also been made in the image of God, as Genesis earlier says? Certainly this teaching is fundamental to biblical values and ethics and, if believed, serves as a generator of mutual respect at all levels of human interaction, beginning in the family.

Could it be that Jacob saw in Esau's generous forgiveness and warmth a reflection of the grace that God had shown him in his life of which not long before he had expressed himself unworthy?

In light of the fact that Jacob had cheated Esau of part of his inheritance, it was also important to him that Esau accept his gift—not so much that it was adequate compensation for the wrong Jacob had done, but because it was a tacit admission of his guilt and an expression of a deep desire to somehow put it right.

Where to go from here? Does this reconciliation presage the brothers' attempt to live together in some sort of commune? Esau, formally at least, suggests that Jacob travel with him and his men, but Jacob politely refuses, though he promises to visit Esau some-time. Jacob may well have recognized that an act of forgiveness and reconciliation between siblings does not necessarily make them compatible companions. Their characters and ways of life were completely different. Neither was perfect but Esau, as the

New Testament points out, in despising his birthright had shown an attitude to God that was essentially profane, so diametrically opposed to Jacob's increasing awareness of the role of God in his life. Any attempt at an expression of unity would eventually have proved artificial and collapsed.

Later years would reveal an ongoing and bitter antagonism between the descendants of Esau—the Edomites—and the people of Israel. Jacob and Esau part. They will not meet again until the death of their father Isaac.

5

Jacob in Shechem; the Violation of Dinah

In the meantime Jacob settled first at Succoth and then Shechem. Genesis next records a very distressing event in the life of the family. Jacob had a daughter, Dinah. (He may well have had more, since it was not normal to record all female descendants as they played no part in inheritance.) Dinah was the daughter of Leah and, up to this point, has played no role in the narrative. But now, we are told, she "went out to see the women of the land" (34:1). As perhaps the only girl in a family of twelve brothers, it was natural for her to seek out female company. There is no mention of anyone going with her. Jacob has clearly put nothing in place to ensure her safety. Inevitably, the local men see her, and one of them in particular, Shechem, who belonged to the princely family of the region, "seized her and lay with her and humiliated her" (34:2). Afterward his attitude toward her changes: "His soul was drawn to Dinah the daughter of Jacob. He loved the young woman and spoke tenderly to her. So Shechem spoke to his father Hamor, saying, 'Get me this girl for my wife'" (34:3–4). So father and son visit Jacob and his sons to plead their case.

As Jacob was trying to settle down in the area, relationships with the locals were of paramount importance, so the men's visit put Jacob in a tricky situation. He had arrived "peacefully" (see marginal reading for 33:18) in the land and had been careful to buy from the local leaders the ground on which his tent was pitched and on which he had erected an altar witnessing to the God of Israel.

Yet Jacob seems to have given no thought as to what would happen to his children when they reached an age when they wished to be married. Both he and his father before him had married relatives from Mesopotamia, and a great fuss was made about them doing so. Yet thus far in the life of Jacob, at least, so far as the text informs us, there has been no reference to Jacob's guiding his children about this issue. But it was a vitally important matter since the developing of this new tribe, the children of Israel, would be dependent on the women who came to join it as spouses for Jacob's children.

Now Jacob was faced with a fait accompli. A delegation of local leaders was asking Jacob to release Dinah to be the wife of their prince. Moreover, they expressed their desire for trade and intermarriage between their tribes. And they asked Jacob to name his bride price for Dinah.

Such suggestions raised all kinds of deep questions that should have been thought out long before. Jacob and his family are now inside the borders of Canaan, the land promised to them by God. But should they intermingle with local pagan tribes in the way now being suggested?

Is this what God intended for them? How would such assimilation affect the uniqueness of their role to represent God in the world? On the other hand, if they were not prepared to assimilate, would it mean they would be driven out by force and, quite possibly, annihilated so that they would lose their role entirely? Such a fraught situation surely demanded wisdom, diplomacy, and, above all, prayer to God as to what should be done.

Yet no one was interested in what God thinks. Jacob's sons, who had joined the group as soon as they heard what was going on, were furious at what had happened to their sister because Shechem "had done an outrageous thing in Israel by lying with Jacob's daughter, for such a thing must not be done" (34:7).

We notice the reference to Israel. Even though the nation was tiny, consisting of just one family, the incident was regarded as having not only moral but political significance. It was an attack on them as a nation.

In their anger the brothers resorted to a cunning and crude strategem. They pretended to agree to the marriage and to the unification of the tribes on the condition that all the local males be circumcised. The foreign delegation agreed and returned to put the matter to their own city leaders, who also agreed, especially when the delegation make the point that, in the end, assimilation would mean, in their view, that all Jacob's tribe's property and livestock would eventually end up in their hands.

The mass circumcision took place with the inevitable consequence that three days later the men were sore and their resistance was at a minimum, as Simeon and Levi had anticipated. The two men took their swords and mercilessly massacred the lot. They then took Dinah back home together with all the spoil they could plunder, including women and children.

Jacob's response left a lot to be desired. He remonstrated with his sons, telling them that their action would bring disaster on the family when the inhabitants of the land heard about it. There is no evidence that he tried to exercise any moral discipline on them, a weak trait that became more evident as he and his sons grew older. Jacob appeared only to be concerned with "I, me, and my." He lamented the fact that his sons' actions had placed him at risk and had made it now impossible for the family to settle in the region.

The sons didn't appear to care and threw the rebuke back in his face with the retort: "Should he treat our sister like a prostitute?" (34:31). They were obviously trying to make a moral and a political point—that the local prince's mistreatment of Dinah, their sister, justified the slaughter of an entire community, to say nothing of carrying off the women and children. The whole situation was so morally grotesque and out of proportion that it is hard not to see beneath it a seething resentment of Jacob and his attitude to them and to Dinah, all of them children of Leah. And what were they going to do with the women they had captured—marry them? It did not bode well for Jacob.

Many parents will recognize in this (admittedly extreme) incident the difficulty—the agonizing difficulty—of trying to cope with a whole raft of problems, with bad behavior in children of a sort that the parents would never have dreamed of engaging in when they themselves were young. Each generation tends to push the boundaries set by the previous one, and it frequently happens that parents, believing parents, find themselves at sea and pushed into moral compromise that leaves them completely bewildered. It is one thing when children are guilty of petty theft; it is another when they commit rape or murder.

The story leaves us with some questions to answer. First, what would you do if someone behaved improperly toward your daughter and either rejected her or wanted to marry her? Second, how should we protect our daughters? Did Jacob even bother telling Dinah, a young unmarried woman, about the dangers of going out on her own into a world where she might not be treated with respect? It is obvious when children are young that we need to keep them physically separate from dangerous situations and places. But when they grow into adults, what then? How can we help them? One thing is clear: it is much easier to talk about discipline than to practice it. Jacob seems to have done neither. Finally, why did God not intervene and tell Jacob what he should have done to avoid the massacre in the first place? Why did God not directly rebuke the cruelty of Jacob's sons?

Our many and pressing questions—usually *why* questions—are not answered in the text, at least not directly. We are simply told what happened. All we can do is think about it and allow it to feed in to our moral compass.

God next speaks to Jacob to tell him to go back to Bethel: "Arise, go up to Bethel and dwell there. Make an altar there to the God who appeared to you when you fled from your brother Esau" (35:1). There is no divine comment on what happened in Shechem, but the very fact that Jacob is told to go somewhere else to live may well indicate that he should not have gone to Shechem in the first place.

Jacob called his family and servants together, and he first commands them: "Put away the foreign gods that are among you and purify yourselves and change your garments" (35:2). It is clear that the group has not kept clear of the influence of the pagan deities around. We recall that even Jacob's wife Rachel stole the household gods from her father Laban as they left. Here Jacob insisted that there must be no compromise in their spiritual allegiance.

He laid out his intentions: "Then let us arise and go up to Bethel, so that I may make there an altar to the God who answers me in the day of my distress and has been with me wherever I have gone" (35:3).

On Jacob's first visit to Bethel, God had appeared to him and promised to go with him. Now Jacob openly acknowledges that God had been true to his word. He also admits that he had been in distress and that God had answered his prayers. It takes courage for a man to admit to feeling distress to his family. Such honesty may be a first step in taking some kind of spiritual lead.

Bethel was due south, on Jacob's way home. But the journey was fraught with peril. The murderous activity of his sons in Shechem had turned the local tribes against him, and Bethel was still in Canaan. The chances of his reaching there, let alone home, were, humanly speaking, very low. He was, however, given superhuman protection: "As they journeyed, a terror from God fell upon the cities that were around them, so that they did not pursue the sons of Jacob" (Gen. 35:5).

It was not so much Jacob but his sons' blood the locals were after, and God stepped in to protect the family. That action raises an obvious question: Why had God not sent a terror earlier to protect Dinah, as he had twice protected Sarah, Abraham's wife? So much tragedy would have been avoided and the current intervention rendered unnecessary. We are not told, but the facts before us show that God does not always do what we might think he should do. His thoughts are not our thoughts, and his ways not our ways.

Jacob was returning to the place he had started from years before. Life had come in a circle, and doubtless he needed time to reflect on all that had happened to him. He was now the patriarch leader of a fledgling nation, a nation chosen by God to play a central role in the Seed Project.

He arrived at Bethel with a great deal of baggage, both literally and metaphorically. What had he really learned in the years since he had left home? He had deceived his father and cheated his brother. In turn, he had been deceived and cheated time and again by his uncle, whom he in turn had deceived and cheated. He had lived with sibling rivalry and tension in his family from the start; he had favoritized one wife to the detriment of the other, and this had spilled over into his attitude toward his children. His children had become immediately insubordinate and even violent as the horrific massacre at Shechem showed. He had failed to protect his daughter.

Was this kind of violence the only way to ensure that the nation remain unified and distinct from the pagan tribes around? And how could stirring up antagonism in this way fulfill God's intention to bring blessing to the world and not only to Israel?

Had Jacob actually achieved anything? He had secured a non-hostility pact with Laban and separated from him. There had been a reconciliation with Esau although each had gone his separate way. Interspersed with all that, Jacob had had sporadic experiences of God speaking to him, of building altars, and of occasionally praying. But it all seems relatively insubstantial apart from the dramatic vision at Bethel and his all-night wrestling at Peniel, when he saw the face of God. That final encounter had left him with a limp that meant he would never forget it.

Yet hard experience had perhaps made Jacob more willing now than he had been the first time around to listen to and take seriously what God would say. And God spoke to him once more, confirming the change of his name to Israel and promising a multitude of descendants in terms of nations and kings. He also promised him yet again the land he gave to Abraham and Isaac.

There was no rebuke regarding his failure to protect his daughter or discipline his sons, no guidance on how to deal with the Canaanites he had antagonized or on where to get spouses for his children. Yet God's statement was full of hope: Israel would become a great nation, and so many of these problems would be solved. That was the message he got when he returned to Bethel.

I cannot help asking myself, and you can ask yourself the same if you wish: Do I need to do the same, to come back to Bethel? This might not be a return in the sense of a physical pilgrimage to a place, though sometimes special places can help us think through issues with which we are concerned. But there is a danger in special places in that we may come to think, for example, that God can only be experienced in a building such as a church. We then lose the sense of God being on our journey with us, ever open for our conversation, ever ready to help direct our paths. The encouragement that God gave to Jacob at Bethel is repeated and written large for us by Jesus in the New Testament: "I will ask the Father, and he will give you another Helper, to be with you forever, even the Spirit of truth" (John 14:16–17). In all the major questions of life, where we often feel overwhelmed and incompetent, we are told to bring them all to God, "casting all [our] anxieties on him, because he cares for [us]" (1 Pet. 5:7).

We are not told how long Jacob stayed at Bethel, nor anything about what he did while he was there. Eventually he started on the final leg of a journey back home to his father Isaac at Hebron.

On the way, a further tragedy hit. Jacob's first love, Rachel, went into a difficult labor, and to Jacob's great sadness, she died giving birth to a son. With her final breath she called her baby Benoni, "son of my sorrow." But Jacob called him Benjamin, "son of my right hand," a full brother for Joseph. This happened near the village Ephrath, or Bethlehem. Jacob buried his wife there by the roadside and set up a pillar that for years afterward was known as the pillar of Rachel's tomb.

Jacob made another stop at Eder where he came to hear of yet another devastating blow to his family. His eldest son, Reuben, whose mother was Leah, had slept with Bilhah, his father's concubine. Bilhah had been Rachel's servant and had given Jacob two sons, Dan and Naphtali. Rachel was now dead. Reuben's deed was outrageous according to the customs of the times, just as Shechem's had been. It amounted to incest and was a direct insult to his father, Jacob, and a challenge to Jacob's authority in the clan. What was Reuben's motivation? Maybe he wished to humiliate his father in revenge for his humiliation of Leah, his mother.

The account of the misdeed is kept short and cryptic. But Jacob did not forget it in his last days when he came to bless his sons, though no action on his part was recorded at the time. Once more there is a total absence of the kind of fatherly interest in obtaining a suitable wife for an eldest son that would have been characteristic of the culture at that time.

Fast-forward to the time of the New Testament where we find Paul having to deal with the very same problem in the church at Corinth: "It is actually reported that there is sexual immorality among you, and of a kind that is not tolerated even among pagans, for a man has his father's wife" (1 Cor. 5:1). The Corinthian church appears to have responded with arrogance, whereas Paul tells them it would have been much more appropriate to mourn. He then insists that they deal with the matter by disciplining the offender and excluding him from their fellowship, at least for a time. Jacob did not. Should he have? What difference, if any, is there between morality before and after the advent of Christianity?

Experience of life tells us that what happened with Reuben and what happened in Corinth can happen today. And that is why the pastoral role in a church is of paramount importance. We should highly value the relatively few men and women who are competent enough to deal with such problems and pray for them constantly. The reputation of the church, and ultimately of God himself, is at stake.

Some time later Jacob arrived home, and just as the preceding section of Genesis ended with the death of Abraham, this section ends by recording the death of Isaac. His sons Jacob and Esau bury him. In chronological terms, it is to be noted that Isaac's death does not actually occur until some years later, when Joseph has spent some time in Egypt. But the writer closes the chapter here with narrative content rather than chronology in his mind.

PART 2

JOSEPH, HIS FATHER, AND HIS BROTHERS

6

Preliminary Considerations

This sixth major section of Genesis, 36:1–50:26, begins with a short section giving a genealogy for Esau and listing many of his descendants. This fits in with the pattern already established with Ishmael and Isaac. Genesis first comments on the son that is not central to the Seed Project and then turns to the son that is. Hence, comments are made about Ishmael before Isaac and here, Esau before Jacob. Genesis 36 is dedicated to Esau and his descendants.

In 37:2 we meet the marker phrase again; this time it refers to Jacob: "These are the generations of Jacob." But instead of finding a list of Jacob's descendants, as we might expect, we simply read: "Joseph, being seventeen years old, was pasturing the flock with his brothers."

At long last we reach the main objective of this book, the story of Joseph. He now plays the prominent role until the end of the book of Genesis. His will be the task to unite his brothers to carry forward the Seed Project. However, we recall from our introduction that the book ends with the death of both Jacob and Joseph, implying that Jacob, although often in the background, is still relevant to the story. We are also told here to read this final narrative as the generations of Jacob, and therefore we should not lose sight of his perspective as we proceed.

In fact, the broadening out of the narrative to include all the sons of Jacob represents a departure in the book of Genesis and distinguishes this final section from those that precede it. Earlier, Genesis records that God made a covenant with Abraham, which was transmitted to one of Abraham's sons, Isaac, and not to the other son, Ishmael. The same pattern of single transmission is repeated with Isaac, where it is Jacob who is chosen to bear the family line and not Esau. But simple logic tells us that there is no way of getting from a single patriarchal founder to a nation that holds to his vision if only one son in each generation is designated to carry the flag. Something radically new has to happen. The new element in the Seed Project is that not a particular chosen one but *all twelve* of the sons of Jacob are to be the founders of an integrated nation.

There is, however, a serious problem right at the start. The brothers' hatred of Joseph because of his dreams of supremacy imperils the project and, far from bringing cohesion to the family, threatens to divide and scatter it irretrievably.

Yet God, through Joseph, achieves a seemingly impossible goal through a process that involves something else that is essentially a new ingredient in Genesis: Joseph's suffering. The story of Joseph has two major phases. First is his lengthy and often painful training that qualifies him to handle great power, and then, second, is his sensitive and skillful use of that power to save the world from starvation and bring about reconciliation with his brothers.

A further new feature of this final section of Genesis is its scale. Abraham, Isaac, and Jacob believed God's promise that he would bless all the nations of the world through them. Yet up to this final stage in the book, we are still talking about a very small nomadic tribal group. The scale is tiny. How can this little family group possibly be relevant to the "blessing" of the wider world? The answer is that in a single dramatic move, Joseph steps from the obscurity of an Egyptian prison directly onto the world stage to bear public witness to the existence of God to Pharaoh.

That witness was so credible that the grateful Pharaoh at once invested Joseph with immense authority, granting him the post of grand vizier of Egypt, second only to Pharaoh himself. Joseph took over the Egyptian ministry of agriculture, where his administrative genius, honed over many years in adverse circumstances, was put to full use in planning for a major famine that would engulf the empire of Egypt and impact regions as far away as Canaan. Genesis began with God creating a world where there is food in abundance. It ends with God sending a man to save a starving world where the harvest has repeatedly failed.

The contours of Joseph's life, fascinating in their own right, as we shall see, also function as a thought model of something even greater. Let us listen to Stephen, the first Christian martyr, defending his faith in Christ before a murderously hostile crowd in Jerusalem. He gives a powerful lesson from the history of Israel, showing that, time and again, the nation's patriarchs resisted the very men that God raised up to save the nation from catastrophe. Stephen points out that God was with Joseph, yet Joseph was rejected by the patriarchs, as later was Moses. Having learned nothing from this, Stephen's audience had shown the very same attitude to the greatest Savior of all, Jesus the Messiah. Stephen's logic was deadly, his message went home, and in yet a further rejection that proved the truth of that message, his hearers stoned him to death (see Acts 6:8–8:2).

This application leads us to expect that in the life of Joseph we shall find certain patterns of behavior that recur at a higher level in the life of our Lord, who came to his own, and his own did not receive him even though he was the Savior of the world and its future King.

But our main concern will be to look at and learn from Joseph's life in its own right. And at this level another biblical comment on Joseph is helpful. It is to be found in one of the psalms that depict events in Israel's history. Speaking of God, the psalmist says:

> When he summoned a famine on the land
>   and broke all supply of bread,
> he had sent a man ahead of them,
>   Joseph, who was sold as a slave.
> His feet were hurt with fetters:
>   his neck was put in a collar of iron;
> until what he had said came to pass,
>   the word of the LORD tested him. (Ps. 105:16–19)

We have seen that the word of God is a central, recurrent theme in Genesis. The word of God was active in creation and in defining the moral relationship between God and humans. According to Genesis, the veracity of the word of God is the first thing that is attacked by the enemy of God: "Did God actually say . . . ?" (Gen. 3:1). And so it has been thereafter. The enemy will do anything, intellectual or moral, to unsettle our confidence in what God has said.

Up to this point in Genesis God has spoken in different ways in direct speech to Adam, Eve, Noah, Abraham, Isaac, and Jacob. What is striking in the story of Joseph is that there is no record of God speaking to him in direct speech. In fact, in the first chapter of Joseph's story, the word "God" does not even appear. Yet, at least with hindsight, we can reasonably say that God did speak to him in two dreams that he had when he was in his teenage years.

No doubt Joseph had heard many accounts from his father about the exploits of the family and the way in which God had dealt with his ancestors. Yet he himself seems to have lived life trusting a God who was mostly silent. The silence of God is a telling phrase, and many people have had to endure something very like it for many years. The words of Psalm 105 form a telling comment on Joseph's quiet yet deep-rooted faith: "Until what he had said came to pass, the word of the LORD tested him."

Sometimes we meet believers whose dealings with God have been dramatic and, apparently, unmistakable. We might, of course, react with skepticism, but we might also react with a feeling of inadequacy if our experience has not been like that. Well, we can derive a deep encouragement from the story of Joseph because the fact that he could be used by God to achieve so much in later life may well be connected with his trust in God *in the absence of the dramatic.*

Joseph held on to what he understood God had indicated to him in his teenage dreams, that one day he would come to power, whatever that meant. As a result, at a crucial moment, he became a powerful public witness for God. This may be the very thing we need to hear in order to help us find the courage to stand publicly for the Lord.

"The Word of the LORD tested him." When engineers are testing materials for use in the space shuttle, wherever possible they subject the materials to laboratory conditions more extreme than they will eventually have to endure in space. Joseph was put under severe pressure in his thirteen-year ordeal of hatred and rejection, slavery, false accusation, and prison. Joseph suffered before he received power and high office. It was a long period of waiting, and yet he held firmly to his faith in God and God's Word all along, even though, we should note, he knew far less of God than we do. His willingness to wait for God's time was amply vindicated.

In that respect Joseph contrasts strongly with Esau to whom Genesis 36 is devoted as part of the background to this final section. There we are told: "These are the kings who reigned in the land of Edom [Esau], before any king reigned over the Israelites" (36:31). Esau wanted to reign, and in the political sense he seems to have done well. Even though he did not gain the blessing of his father, nonetheless, as God had said, he thrived. Yet there seems to be something missing. There is not a single hint of any interest in a spiritual dimension. This is confirmed by the New Testament, which says the following about Esau:

> See to it that no one . . . is sexually immoral or unholy like Esau, who sold his birthright for a single meal. (Heb. 12:15–16)

Esau's philosophy was made clear when he sold his birthright to Jacob for a plate of stew: immediate satisfaction of his appetite for food with no sense of the importance of his intangible birthright. Hebrews talks about Esau in the context of sexual immorality, which also is characterized by the same attitude—satisfaction of the appetite now, no matter what the consequences, no matter what parameters God may have set down about it. Nothing is sacred for the man who is driven by immediate satisfaction of his desires.

There were kings in Edom before there were kings in Israel. Yet Joseph came to reign in a way that Esau never did, because in the Bible, the way to get real authority is a pathway that Esau was not prepared to follow. "If we endure," says the New Testament, "we will also reign with him" (2 Tim. 2:12).

The apostle Peter wrote to Christians to prepare them for the pressure, harassment, and persecution that he saw coming. Peter pointed them to Christ and what his path was predicted to be by the prophets. The prophets talked about the sufferings of Christ and the glories that should *follow* those sufferings (1 Pet. 1:11). For Christ the path was first suffering and then glory. At the end of his letter Peter says,

> Humble yourselves, therefore, under the mighty hand of God so that at the proper time he may exalt you, casting all your anxieties on him, because he cares for you. Be sober-minded; be watchful. Your adversary the devil prowls around like a roaring lion, seeking someone to devour. Resist him, firm in your faith, knowing that the same kinds of suffering are being experienced by your brotherhood throughout the world. And after you have suffered a little while, the God of all grace, who has called you to his eternal glory in Christ, will himself restore, confirm, strengthen, and establish you. (1 Pet. 5:6–10)

The pathway for Christ was suffering before glory. Joseph becomes a deeply instructive embodiment of it.

7

The Genesis of Hatred

To everyone there belongs a biography. There are reasons why we are as we are. If the Bible told us stories only of people who came from good backgrounds and developed into strong men and women of God, most of us would end up being very discouraged. But it doesn't. The Bible talks about life as it really is: petty, messy, full of strained relationships, dysfunctional, unfair, and sometimes even murderously violent. That is what life was like for Joseph growing up in Jacob's family, with its two wives and two further surrogate mothers so that there were in the family one husband and four "wives," with thirteen children distributed among them.

The family contained all the ingredients for a psychological nightmare.

The narrative now concentrates on three primary issues that combined to generate deep antagonism between the brothers and Joseph:

1. Joseph brought a bad report about the sons of the two surrogate mothers.
2. Jacob openly treated Joseph as his favorite son.
3. Joseph had dreams of supremacy over his brothers and parents and related them to his family.

1. A Bad Report

The story begins with Joseph, seventeen years old, working as a shepherd with his brothers. The brilliant Jewish commentator Leon Kass (professor emeritus on the Committee of Social Thought at the University of Chicago, and chairman of the Presidential Council on Bioethics from 2001–2005), suggests that Genesis 37:2 should read: "Joseph, being seventeen years old, was shepherding his brothers among the flock." Kass describes Joseph as "*at best* a spy reporting on request to his father about the deeds of the brothers he was 'shepherding'" and possibly exaggerating his report to ingratiate himself with his father.[1] However, other scholars point out that the story of Joseph as a whole gives no evidence that he had such a character flaw, although it reveals character flaws in his brothers that demonstrate that Joseph's reports may well have been accurate. It also appears that Jacob could trust Joseph but not them.

It may well have been more complex. We are told here that Joseph was his father's favorite son, being the firstborn of Jacob's first love. Apart from his younger brother Benjamin, the rest of Jacob's sons were Joseph's half-brothers and somewhat older than he was. We cannot, of course, assume that Joseph had no character flaws whatsoever; he, like all the rest of us, was not sinless. In addition, a favorite child—indeed, any child—can be tempted to tell tales to enhance his or her position in the family pecking order. How often children threaten their siblings with, "Just you watch it, or I'll tell on you."

It would rather strain our credulity to think that basking in the favoritism of his father had no negative effect on Joseph in terms of overconfidence and self-righteousness tinged with arrogance. Child psychologist Gaynor Sbuttoni says that even the favored child suffers in the long run: "As soon as children become aware of the favouritism, sibling rivalry is intensified to an almost

---

1. Leon Kass, *The Beginning of Wisdom: Reading Genesis* (New York: Free Press, 2003), 513.

intolerable level. On top of that, the preferred child's own sense of worth is undermined by praise which is not individual, but tailored to be an odious comparison."[2]

Yet whatever the degree to which such things characterized Joseph's late teens, we may be sure that life's experiences would be used by God to refine him. We can also observe that the Bible has much to say about the potentially dangerous consequences of doing what Joseph did, talebearing, whatever its motivation. The Lord warned through Moses: "You shall not go around as a slanderer among your people, and you shall not stand up against the life of your neighbor: I am the LORD" (Lev. 19:16).

Telling tales and gossiping have virtually unlimited capacity to destroy relationships in families, churches, and organizations of any kind. The context of this biblical prohibition on talebearing is this: "You shall not take vengeance or bear a grudge against the sons of your own people, but you shall love your neighbor as yourself" (Lev. 19:18).

This suggests that refraining from telling tales is an expression of loving your neighbor as yourself. Let us do a simple thought experiment. Suppose we were to identify in all of our conversations of the past week everything we had said about other people. We might wonder, first, what proportion it would form of all that we have said—ten percent, or maybe more than fifty? Second, we might ask how much of what we said about others was completely correct. Suppose God were to take all that we have said about other people in the last week and apply the principles that we have applied to analyze other people's lives to analyze our lives. What would the result be? It might be so unpleasant that it does not bear contemplation. Yet we should think about it since something like that is inevitably going to happen one day. Now, one of the glorious things about the gospel is

2. Gaynor Sbuttoni, "Do All Your Kids a Favour," *The Guardian*, October 9, 2002, accessed November 7, 2018, https://www.theguardian.com/lifeandstyle/2002/oct/09/family andrelationships.features10.

that we are saved from the penalty of our sins, and in that sense we shall never come into judgment; we have passed from death to life. But, as Paul points out, all Christians must face not the final judgment but the judgment seat of Christ so that they may receive for the deeds done in the body.

We are all going to be assessed, but not to determine whether we will get into the kingdom of God, for salvation is not of works but apart from works, by grace through faith in Christ. We shall be assessed at the judgment seat of Christ in order to determine our reward. The Scripture is quite clear on it. And one of the ways we are going to be assessed is this: "With the measure you use it will be measured back to you," said Christ (Luke 6:38).

Idle talk is destructive. It is so easy for any of us to give in to the temptation to share some juicy gossip, of course with the proviso: "Please don't tell anybody, because I promised not to tell anybody." That's an impressive bit of moral logic, isn't it? And who of us is innocent?

There is an obvious lesson for us all in this. And there is another reason why it is important. There are many people, particularly but not only young people, who long to find someone with whom they can share their deepest and most worrying problems in the knowledge that what they say will be kept confidential. Are we such people? We ought to strive to be.

Rather than judging Joseph, we might be wiser to look within our own hearts, for there is another possibility. From what we know of his brothers, Joseph's reports might well have contained a considerable element of truth. The martyr Stephen, as we saw, draws a parallel between the patriarchs' rejection of Joseph and the rejection of the Lord Jesus. Why was Jesus rejected? As recorded by John, the brothers of Jesus once said to him: "No one works in secret if he seeks to be known openly. If you do these things, show yourself to the world." And Jesus replied, "My time has not yet come, but your time is always here" (John 7:4, 6). And in the midst of his remarks he identified the problem: "The world cannot hate you, but it hates me because I testify about it that its works are evil" (7:7).

It is wrong to be a talebearer. But, and I am sure we have all felt the difficulty here, we are called upon to preach a message that concerns God's attitude to sin, and this will inevitably produce antagonism. In one of my debates with Richard Dawkins, he belittled all concern about sin. But sin is serious; it destroys our civilizations, and it can destroy us. We have to talk about it.

However, because we are not perfect like our Lord, we need to be careful as to how we do that. It is so easy to fail to recognize that we ourselves are sinners and speak of sin in such a superior, moralizing way that we simply antagonize people. For the very same reason, it is also not difficult to avoid talking about sin altogether. We are given neither option.

I once heard a story of how two Christians were called to help someone whose life was in a mess. On the way, the older of the two asked his companion: "Do you think you could have done what he did?" And the younger replied, "Oh, no, I couldn't have done that." The older then said: "Well, you just go home, and I shall see him on my own." The man had to be seen and confronted with painful issues in order to be helped. But the only one who was qualified to do that was the one who had no illusions about his own frailty and sin.

Whatever motive we ascribe to Joseph's behavior, we know that the report he gave to his father was at least one of the things that fueled his brothers' hatred of him. And it is not possible to leave this issue without raising the related matter of whistle-blowing. Many companies and industries have, in their own interests and those of their employees, set up whistle-blowing policies. The wrongdoing you disclose must be in the public interest.

But there was a further matter that incensed the brothers.

2. Jacob's Favoritism

Jacob loved Joseph, which is good for a father to do, but the problem was that he loved Joseph more than his other sons.

Another problem was that Jacob didn't keep his preference under control but expressed it by giving Joseph a magnificent robe, a many-colored robe that distinguished him visibly from the other brothers. Moreover, such a robe in that culture may well have been associated with authority and leadership. It would have been taken as a symbol of Jacob's designation of Joseph as the (potential) clan leader. It had the effect of pouring gasoline on the flames of the brothers' hatred.

Jacob of all people should have known better and should have seen that this was an unwise move. He had himself been born into a family split over who loved whom and why. Isaac, his father, loved Esau because he was his type of outdoor man, and Rebekah loved Jacob. This rivalry led to endless problems. Yet, as often happens, Jacob didn't profit from his own experience. In consequence he was condemned to see his preference for Joseph cause bitter and far-reaching dissension that wrought havoc with his family relationships over many years.

Some of us may have Jacob's problem. When children are small, they do not occupy much space, though they may occupy a lot of time and attention. But gradually those of us who are parents become aware that our space and time are increasingly filled by powerful young minds, hearts, and wills—all of them different from each other and from us. Some are agreeable and others problematic, if not downright difficult. It is so easy then to favor the children that are like us and to distance ourselves from those who are unlike us. We may, of course, struggle to be fair. But we sometimes fail, if not in our own eyes then in those of our children, don't we? And some of our parents failed too. We may have been like Joseph and felt the glow of basking in a parent's smile and may also have suffered the consequences because our siblings were not treated in the same way. Or we may have been like Joseph's brothers and known how hard it is not to be the favorite. As a result, we may still be dealing with resentment. Our parents may be long gone, but the family is still torn apart by old resentments, envies, and tensions.

Just think, for example, of how many families you know, whether Christian or not, who are at war over family legacies.

C. S. Lewis points out in a famous essay how proud we can become as adults, even in Christian circles, when we get into the "inner ring," and how desolated we can be when we are left out of it.[3] These are very real things, aren't they? All of us are affected by them. Indeed, many of us are struggling with them right now. In Jacob's day, at a human level, his action threatened God's plan to have a nation that faithfully witnessed to him in the world. Today such issues constantly threaten our families, our churches, and our workplaces, and they imperil our witness to the world. That is why it is important that we face what Scripture teaches—some principles from Scripture—and do something about them.

God Is Impartial

Jacob took a long time to grasp this. He imagined that because God had given him a special role in the Seed Project, it didn't matter very much how he behaved. He had to learn the hard way that God has no favorites. God had to teach him that to be chosen for a special role did not mean that God would approve of Jacob's questionable corner-cutting methods of achieving his, or even God's, objectives for his life. Indeed, God has the right to expect better things from us, does he not? The apostle Peter explains this to us by spelling out the implications of calling on God as Father, who, unlike Jacob, is utterly impartial:

> "Be holy, for I am holy." And if you call on him as Father who judges impartially according to each one's deeds, conduct yourself with fear throughout the time of your exile, knowing that you were ransomed from the futile ways inherited from your forefathers, not with perishable things such as silver and gold, but with the precious blood of Christ, like that of a lamb without blemish or spot. (1 Pet. 1:16–19)

---

3. C. S. Lewis, *The Screwtape Letters* (New York: Bantam, 1995), 72.

If we were given a car as a gift to help us out when we couldn't afford to buy one, we would be churlish and ungrateful to complain to the giver the first time anything went wrong with it. If, on the other hand, we spent good money at a car dealership for a car that proved to have a serious fault on the first day, we would certainly complain to the dealer and feel we had a right to do so. We paid for it, so we expect it to run well.

This is Peter's logic. You and I, if we are believers in Christ, have had a great deal spent on us. We have not been redeemed with corruptible things, such as silver and gold, but by the most expensive currency in the universe: *the blood of Christ that was given for us.* Since God has spent so much on us, he surely has the right to expect something from our lives, does he not?

But there is something else. There is a person we can come to if we have sinned by being partial or talebearing or hurtful in what we have said—Jesus our Savior and Lord: "If we confess our sins, he is faithful and just to forgive us our sins and to cleanse us from all unrighteousness" (1 John 1:9). He alone can enable us to get up again and face the next day.

Be Impartial

Partiality may rear its head in leadership situations. In this connection Paul tells Timothy that, on the one hand, no charge against a leader should be admitted except on the evidence of two or three witnesses (1 Tim. 5:19–23). On the other hand, Timothy must be prepared to rebuke in the presence of all those leaders who persist in sin so that the rest may stand in fear.

That was a tough call. Timothy, like some of us, was a nervous man, indeed so nervous that Paul once had to write to a church to encourage its members to see to it that Timothy was among them without fear. Timothy was prone to timidity and that awful feeling in the stomach that went with it, which is why Paul advised him to take a glass of wine from time to time. And if you are nervous, it is very easy to give in to a powerful pressure group and show partiality. How can you help a Timothy to be impartial? By reminding him of who is watching. Paul says: "In the presence of God and of Christ Jesus and of the elect angels I charge you to keep these rules without prejudging, doing nothing from partiality" (1 Tim. 5:21).

If there is a lot of pressure to show favoritism, says Paul to Timothy, it will help you to remember just who is watching: God is watching, Christ is watching, and the elect angels are watching. If ever there was a statement guaranteed to encourage people to make the right decision, it is that. Someone has defined character as what we are like when no one sees. But there is never a situation when no one sees!

Joseph was presented with the coat, and no doubt his father proudly insisted that he try it on and show it off to the family. There is no hint of any awareness on Jacob's part that he was repeating his own parents' mistake. Nor is there any sign of Joseph thinking twice before he wore the coat in front of his brothers and by doing so increased his already tense relationships with his brothers.

Jacob's error was to give an expensive piece of clothing to one of his children that he did not also give to the others. That can easily happen today, so those of us who are parents need to be very careful here. Children are also under pressure at school and college, where it is well known that they can be bullied for wearing the wrong gear. Joseph was bullied for wearing the expensive cloak given him by his father. But what do we do as parents if our children are bullied for not wearing the latest in expensive athletic shoes, jeans, or T-shirts? A quick search of the Internet shows that many parents face these problems and understand their child's desire to look good but try to accommodate that by careful searching for clothes that do look attractive but are not too expensive. Some think it is a good idea for parents, if they can afford it, to allow a child to have one good brand-name item but also suggest it should be given on a special occasion, for birthday or Christmas, for instance.

Those of us who are Christians need to think this out carefully since we wish to teach our children that their value does not reside in the cost of their clothes. We do not wish to overindulge them, but neither do we wish to expose them to bullying, nor do we wish to alienate them from us. As soon as we can, we need to have open discussions about these issues.

It would have been difficult for Joseph as a boy to suppress pride at being his father's favorite, and one can readily imagine that it led to resentment, spite, jealousy, and, in the end, hatred on the part of his brothers.

3. Joseph's Dreams

Worse was to come—and quickly.

> Now Joseph had a dream, and when he told it to his brothers they hated him even more. He said to them, "Hear this dream that I have dreamed: Behold, we were binding sheaves in the field, and behold, my sheaf arose and stood upright. And behold, your sheaves gathered around it and bowed down to my sheaf." His brothers said to him, "Are you indeed to reign over us? Or are you indeed to rule over us?" So they hated him even more for his dreams and for his words.
>
> Then he dreamed another dream and told it to his brothers and said, "Behold, I have dreamed another dream. Behold, the sun, the moon, and eleven stars were bowing down to me." But when he told it to his father and to his brothers, his father rebuked him and said to him, "What is this dream that you have dreamed? Shall I and your mother and your brothers indeed come to bow ourselves to the ground before you?" And his brothers were jealous of him, but his father kept the saying in mind. (Gen. 37:5–11)

This is the first time in Scripture we are told that a person *had a dream*. Earlier we read of God appearing to people in a dream, but that is not the case here, although it later becomes clear that

Joseph at some stage, perhaps the very beginning, came to believe that God had sent his dreams.

There is an important difference between dreams that owe their origin to God and dreams that are produced by subconscious mental activity. Paul warns us about this: "Let no one disqualify you . . . going on in detail about visions, puffed up without reason by [a] sensuous mind, and not holding fast to the Head" (Col. 2:18). Such people really are seeing things. Something is going on in their heads, but they are out of touch with reality; they are not holding fast to the Head.

It is one thing when God sends dreams; it is a completely different thing when people imagine that every dream that they have has some kind of spiritual significance so that in the end they unbalance and become more interested in their dreams than in reading Scripture and praying. Such imaginings can lead to spiritual and moral shipwreck. I can well recall while at university there was a man who sold his Bible, saying he did not need it since God communicated with him in dreams and visions and told him what to do: this, very sadly, included leaving his wife.

Also, although dreams do occur in the Joseph narrative, one of the most striking things is that God could have, at any time, saved many people from long, drawn-out pain and distress by speaking to them in a dream. For instance, God could have sent Jacob a dream that Joseph was still alive, couldn't he? But he didn't. Joseph could have had another dream explaining in more detail what was going to happen. But he didn't.

God sent the dream. That wasn't Joseph's fault. Then Joseph told it to his family. Was that wise? Why didn't he keep it to himself and save himself a lot of trouble? Once more, opinion is divided as to Joseph's motivation. Some think that, driven by ambition, he told the dream to spite his brothers and make them envious. Some skeptics go further and think that Joseph's dreams are simply a projection of his own ambitions. Yet others remind us that Joseph lived in a culture and a family in which dreams had played a role in the past, and, because he was only seventeen, he told the dream in an unguarded natural way as something of interest that had happened to him. After all, the first dream concerned sheaves of corn, and the brothers were cattle men. What could it possibly mean?

The problem was, of course, that at one level the meaning of the two dreams was blindingly obvious. In his dream Joseph had seen his brothers' sheaves bowing to his, and, in an intensification of the same message, the second dream was about the sun, moon, and eleven stars bowing to him. There was no indication of how and when all this might happen and what exactly it would involve. But the basic thrust was clear.

The dreams were clearly meant to predict Joseph's eventual rule over his brothers and indeed over his father and mother, an outrageously unthinkable idea in Middle Eastern culture. One can imagine that it was not in the most even of tones that Jacob said, "Shall I and your mother and your brothers indeed come to bow ourselves to the ground before you?"

It all made Jacob deeply thoughtful. It may well have reminded him that many years before, he had had a dream of a ladder from earth to heaven accompanied by a promise from God to go with him. His dream had come true. Perhaps God had something special in mind for his favorite son, although Joseph's dream seemed to indicate an authority even beyond that of his father. One wonders if Jacob discussed it with Joseph at the time.

Joseph's relating of his dream made the brothers very angry. It also made them jealous, which indicates that they, too—perhaps deep down—recognized there was something substantive at the back of it all. Their fury broke the surface, and they taunted Joseph sarcastically: "Are you indeed to reign over us?"

It was irritating enough to have Joseph parade in front of them with his hateful cloak. It was maddening to listen to his dreams of power and authority over them.

They simply couldn't handle the idea, so preposterous did it seem. One day they would have to handle the reality of confronting that power, as would Joseph have to learn to handle the possession of it.

Their very language here reminds us of a similar attitude displayed centuries later to the Lord Jesus. His mother, Mary, was told by the angel Gabriel something that infinitely eclipses anything contained in Joseph's dream. The angel told her that "the Lord God will give to him [Jesus] the throne of his father David, and he will reign over the house of Jacob forever, and of his kingdom there will be no end" (Luke 1:32–33). Jesus was a descendant of Jacob and yet was to rule over Jacob.

Joseph's brothers did not believe that he would rule over them one day. We can understand that, because at that early stage there was no corroborating evidence to justify Joseph's claim. Many years would pass before they would obtain it.

Jesus's claim to be the Lord, the Son of God, provoked such hostility that eventually the leaders of the nation crucified him, screaming their hatred: "We do not want this man to reign over us" (Luke 19:14).

But precisely because of that cross, millions have bowed the knee, and out of those millions God has formed his church. Those who crucified Jesus hated the fact that he was special, because they did not understand what that meant. Likewise Joseph's brothers. They had no idea that the fulfillment of the dream that fired their hatred would be central to their salvation. And the irony is that they would never understand it until they willingly did what they swore never to do: bow down to Joseph.

8

The Brothers' Revenge

In spite of the obvious tension in the family and the growing hatred, of which Jacob must have been fully aware, he foolishly decided to send Joseph to see how the brothers were faring. That wasn't easy for Joseph. He knew the brothers hated him. He knew it was dangerous, but he still agreed to go, on his own, as far as we can tell—a seventeen-year-old without any company or protection, sent to hostile brothers and into hostile territory. What was Jacob thinking? He hadn't protected his daughter Dinah, and now, even though perfectly aware of the justifiable Canaanite hostility to his family that resulted from her rape, he didn't even bother to protect his favorite son from the Canaanites, let alone from his brothers. Jacob would have plenty of time to regret his action. As Joseph left home, little did Jacob think that he would not see his son again for twenty years.

After walking for over fifty miles Joseph arrived in Shechem where his brothers were supposed to be. They were not there. Joseph found out where they were only by bumping into a man who had overheard them discussing their plans. They had, in fact, moved several miles on from Shechem to a place called Dothan.

It was one of those apparent accidents that changed the course of history. There are several in this story, and they remind us of the subtle way in which God is in control even though we do not always perceive it. Far from being sheer happenstance, we can surely see in such events God's providential government, which interacts in a mysterious, unfathomable way with our human freedom and responsibility.

Paul addressed this matter in his lecture to the Athenian philosophers, some of whom were determinists and others those who believed that chance was king: "And he made from one man every nation of mankind to live on all the face of the earth, having determined allotted periods and the boundaries of their dwelling place, that they should seek God, and perhaps feel their way toward him and find him" (Acts 17:26–27).

It is sad when some people with the best of motives, eager to protect the doctrine of the sovereignty of God, forget the glory of God's genius in creating human beings capable of responding to him in trust and obedience. It is equally sad when others so stress human freedom that they make no space for the glory of God's providence. There is much in Genesis about both, as Paul himself tells us in Romans 9–11.[1]

The brothers watched Joseph approach and saw their chance of getting rid of him. Like Jesus centuries later, Joseph was coming to his own, and his own were about to reject him. "They said to one another, 'Here comes this dreamer. Come now, let us kill him . . . and we will see what becomes of his dreams'" (Gen. 37:19–20). It was no idle talk. Levi and Simeon had proved themselves capable of multiple murders to defend their sister. They had justified it in the name of protecting the family. And now? They planned to murder their brother. Even their family was not sacrosanct.

Joseph had taken a long journey to see how his brothers were faring so he could bring a report to his father. But they were tired of his reports. They would ensure that there would be no more, ever. But they did not all feel the same about what was to be done

---

1. See my *Determined to Believe?: The Sovereignty of God, Freedom, Faith, and Human Responsibility* (Oxford, UK: Lion Hudson, 2017).

to Joseph. At least one, Reuben, the eldest, very different from Simeon and Levi, was touched by some element of compassion and attempted to buy time for Joseph. He hoped he could work out a way to save him and take him back to Jacob. Reuben may even have been full of guilt because of the earlier insult he had paid to Jacob and may have wished to do something to make his father look more favorably on him.

For whatever reason, he said to his brothers: "Let us not take his life. . . . Shed no blood; throw him into this pit here in the wilderness, but do not lay a hand on him" (37:21–22). Reuben said this to rescue Joseph from them and take him back to his father. The brothers were intent on murder, but something in what Reuben said held them back, so when Joseph arrived, they seized him, stripped him of the robe that they hated, and threw him into the water cistern, which happened to be dry at the time. One cannot help thinking of what happened centuries later when another expensive robe was stripped from Jesus when they seized him to make sport of him and torture him.

Joseph's multicolored coat would protect him no longer. Nor would his father. It must have been a horrific shock to realize that he had seriously underestimated his brothers' hostility, and he was clearly going to suffer, even die, for it. He was terrified.

Such cisterns, hollowed out in the ground, were usually bottle shaped with the neck at the top, and it would therefore have been impossible for Joseph to climb out. The brothers then sat around the rim at the top of the cistern and callously ate their food, while inside the cistern their teenage brother cried his heart out, as they later recalled with bitter regret: "We saw the distress of his soul, when he begged us and we did not listen" (42:21).

After throwing Joseph into the cistern, they spotted a caravan in the distance. The camel drivers were Ishmaelites and therefore descendents of Abraham and thus distantly related to the brothers. They were on their way down to Egypt to trade. That gave Judah an idea. Judah, who will eventually play a key role in this story and in world history, said: "What profit is it if we kill our brother and conceal his blood? Come, let us sell him to the Ishmaelites, and let not our hand be upon him, for he is our brother, our own flesh" (37:26–27).

Judah's brothers listened to him rather than stick with Reuben's suggestion. Reuben was the firstborn and therefore the natural heir and leader of the family. By listening to Judah they were effectively rejecting Reuben's leadership. Accordingly, they bargained with the Ishmaelite traders and sold Joseph for twenty shekels of silver.

Judah shows just the bare remnants of humanity. He stops short of fratricide when he sees a way of getting rid of Joseph without killing him and making a profit at the same time. It is enough to save Joseph's life.

Their hated brother has become a commodity, a slave, one more in the pathetic, shuffling millions of men and women who have been demeaned by their fellow men and women and consigned to the inhumanity of slavery. It will take amazing grace to rescue Judah and his brothers, just as it took amazing grace to rescue the slave trader John Newton in 1748, the man who wrote the much-loved hymn to celebrate that grace and who profoundly influenced that magnificent liberator of slaves, William Wilberforce. But all of that was yet a long time in the future.

They sold their brother. The price they were paid is evidence for the historicity of the account, since ancient records show that it matches the going rate for slaves at the time. K. A. Kitchen dates it to the eighteenth century BC.[2] Judah's action also reminds us of another man, Judas (which is a Hellenized version of Judah), who betrayed the Savior of the world for thirty pieces of silver—a Savior who is otherwise, and remarkably, known as the Lion of the tribe of Judah. He also was a descendant of Judah. But that sale was to ensure a death, not to preserve a life.

---

2. K. A. Kitchen, *Ancient Orient and Old Testament* (London: Tyndale Press, 1966), 53.

For some reason Reuben was absent when the brothers sold Joseph and was devastated when he found the boy gone. His behavior could lead us to imagine that Reuben was an unreliable man who seemed incapable of following anything through, even though the life of his brother depended on it. He tore his clothes in despair and found his remaining brothers: "The boy is gone, and I, where shall I go?" (37:30).

We are not told how Reuben responded to the news that Joseph was on his way to Egypt. We are simply informed what the brothers decided to do in order to convince Jacob that Joseph was dead and that they'd had nothing to do with it. We can well imagine that Reuben's conscience tortured him, as he was, in the end, forced by the sheer intensity of the others' hatred of Joseph to go along with the deception. His guilt would take many years to break through to the surface.

They stripped Joseph of his expensive coat, the symbol of all they despised, and dipped it in the blood of a goat they had killed. It was time to go home and present their "findings" to Jacob. The journey would have taken a few days, and there is no record of it or of any dissension along the way. They then showed the blood-stained coat to Jacob: "This we have found; please identify whether it is your son's robe or not" (37:32). Jacob is deceived into believing that his favorite son was dead. He had no way of telling the difference between human and animal blood, as we do now. He accepts the evidence, not knowing it to be false. Heartbroken, he mourns and, in utter hypocrisy, his children unite to "comfort" him.

There is a deeper issue here. Jacob was deceived by a coat dipped in the blood of a goat. Years before, Jacob, whose name, we recall, means "deceiver," dressed himself in a coat of goat's skin at the suggestion of his mother Rebekah so that, if his father were to touch him, he would mistake him for Esau, his hairy brother. The deception convinced Isaac, who accepted the false evidence that Jacob presented. Now it is Jacob himself who is being deceived by his sons presenting false evidence, Joseph's coat dipped in goat's blood.

It is not hard to see that we have here a telling example of how God registered his disapproval of the methods that Jacob used to steal the blessing from Isaac. Jacob eventually found himself on the receiving end of the same kind of fraud that he himself had been happy to perpetrate so many years before. It is another outworking of this principle: "With the measure you use it will be measured back to you" (see, e.g., Luke 6:38).

Jacob had to endure the bitter fruit of his sons' deceit for many years, during which time God did nothing to alleviate his pain. As we said earlier, God could have appeared to Jacob at any time and told him that Joseph was still alive. But God remained silent. He insists that we learn our lessons, whether we are believers or not. That can be tough, very tough. There may be a lesson in this for us. Sometimes the circumstances through which we are going prompt memories of similar circumstances in the past. It is worth then pausing to see if there is anything we can learn from it, for example, if we are in imminent danger of repeating past mistakes. Jacob failed to do that.

Jacob's family has begun to disintegrate; he has lost one son, his favorite. His loss will soon be made greater.

The sons also maintained their conspiracy of silence for years. Suppressing the truth for a long time is not easy to do, and yet so many people manage to do it—Christians included. I have noticed in many families that there are old people clearly disturbed in their consciences by long-buried secrets that they have never been able to face. Sometimes it involves others who know about it but more often than not, it has to do with the covering up of something in their past of which they are ashamed. Their sense of guilt robs them of peace and joy and can often lead to emotional and even physical disorders. Although they would say that they believe the gospel, they nevertheless do not seem to have grasped the nature of God's forgiveness upon repentance, a subject on which the later experience of Joseph with his brothers will throw real light.

For the moment, though, it may be that reading this paragraph causes you a prick of conscience in your heart and reminds you of a buried guilt that you would love to be rid of. You may feel like King David:

> For when I kept silent, my bones wasted away
>> through my groaning all day long.
> For day and night your hand was heavy upon me;
>> my strength was dried up as by the heat of summer.
>
> I acknowledged my sin to you,
>> and I did not cover my iniquity;
> I said, "I will confess my transgressions to the LORD,"
>> and you forgave the iniquity of my sin. (Ps. 32:3–5)

The New Testament says the same to Christians:

> This is the message we have heard from him and proclaim to you, that God is light, and in him is no darkness at all. If we say we have fellowship with him while we walk in darkness, we lie and do not practice the truth. But if we walk in the light, as he is in the light, we have fellowship with one another, and the blood of Jesus his Son cleanses us from all sin. If we say we have no sin, we deceive ourselves, and the truth is not in us. *If we confess our sins, he is faithful and just to forgive us our sins and to cleanse us from all unrighteousness.* If we say we have not sinned, we make him a liar, and his word is not in us. (1 John 1:5–10)

Confession and forgiveness can bring peace and new joy, as King David discovered:

> Blessed is the one whose transgression is forgiven,
>> whose sin is covered.
> Blessed is the man against whom the LORD counts no
>> iniquity,
> and in whose spirit there is no deceit. (Ps. 32:1–3)

It is hard to imagine what it must have been like for a teenage boy to be so hated by his brothers that they first plan to murder him and then settle for selling him into slavery. Joseph, still only a teenager, found himself being carried along in an Ishmaelite caravan traveling south to Egypt. Unlike Judah, who, we will see later, "went down" from his family voluntarily (Gen. 38:1), Joseph was "brought down" by strangers intent on selling him into slavery for the best price.

He would surely have known who the Ishmaelites were through the constant retelling of the major events in family history. For instance, he would have been aware that Ishmael, who was a son of Abraham, had been cast out by his father. That would have been a powerful reason for Joseph not to let his captors know precisely who he was and give them the opportunity of making his predicament even worse. Now he was in Ishmael's power on his way to an alien country with a totally different culture and language.

Think of his feelings as he arrived at a slave market where men and women were openly paraded and sold like cattle to the highest bidder. It immediately makes us ask how this man, young and alone, will maintain the vision. He is now about two hundred miles from home, surrounded by an alien world. How will he keep alive his faith in God, when some of us find it difficult in much easier situations?

The Ishmaelites sell Joseph in the slave market to one of Pharaoh's senior officers, the captain of the Egyptian imperial guard, a man called Potiphar.

9

Judah's Family Life

We are now left in suspense regarding what happens to Joseph, while the narrative turns to one of the other main players in this drama, Judah, the fourth son of Jacob, born to Leah, the apparently less attractive of the two daughters of Laban. Judah, we have learned, was the man who suggested selling Joseph into slavery—a man, apparently, without a heart.

Yet God is interested in Judah even though at this stage Judah appears to show no interest in God. In particular, God is concerned about Judah's family line, just as God has been concerned from the beginning of this book for the offspring of the woman that shall bruise the Serpent's head (Gen. 3:15), a seed that is to be traced through Abraham, Isaac, Jacob, and, now, amazingly, Judah. This story will discuss Judah's attitude to the preservation of his own family line.

We are not told why Judah left home. The text laconically says that he "went down from his brothers" (38:1), inviting us to think that this may well have been true in more senses than one. Judah may well have felt that he had had enough of parental restriction, that he needed to get out and breathe some fresh air. He may also have had a troubled conscience over Joseph and wanted to get away from being constantly reminded of it by his coconspirators.

Whatever the reason, Judah left home, leaving Jacob's family (as he thought at the time) depleted by two sons. Family disintegration was setting in.

We recall that some of the brothers had been involved in a horrific crime of deceit, violence, and murder against a Canaanite group at Shechem. Despite that, Judah shows more interest in Canaanite culture than he does in his own. This is a bad sign, for it makes even more difficult the founding of a family committed to God, let alone a nation. Judah has no interest in the careful seeking of a Hebrew wife, as did his grandfather and father. He simply saw and took a Canaanite woman and had three sons by her: Er, Onan, and Shelah. Judah finds a wife, Tamar, for Er. But Judah's son turns out to be an evil man. Er was wicked, so wicked that the Lord killed him.

Here we encounter the disturbing fact that God, on rare occasions, may intervene to terminate a human life because of serious evil. It happened at this point, and it happened in the New Testament times, for instance, in Jerusalem with Ananias and Sapphira (see Acts 5) and, as Paul tells us, in the church at Corinth (1 Cor. 11:30).

Judah insisted that his second son should act according to what was later termed the "Levirate law" and raise up children to the first son's wife in order to maintain the family line. Onan refuses and the Lord executes him as well. It is not only Jacob who is losing his family but now Judah as well. Two of his three sons are dead, and Judah's, and therefore Jacob's, family succession is in serious danger of terminating.

In a half-hearted attempt to do something about it, Judah said to his daughter-in-law, Tamar: "Remain a widow in your father's house, till Shelah my son grows up" (Gen. 38:11). Marriage to Shelah was her right under the aforementioned Levirate law. However, when the time came for the marriage, Judah failed to keep his promise.

Judah also denies another value very important to Israel: care for his widowed daughter-in-law. His family line is in grave danger of petering out, and he does not seem to be concerned about it.

To cap it all, Judah's wife dies. He is left with one young son and a presumably much older daughter-in-law, Tamar.

However, Tamar does care about the family line and resorts to a desperate strategem. She knows her father-in-law's sexual proclivities and sets about exploiting them. She dresses as a prostitute and sits where she knows that Judah will pass by. Judah sees her, and, deceived by her clothes, fails to recognize who she is. Think back to the deception that Judah and his brothers had perpetrated on Jacob using Joseph's clothes. Now Judah, unwittingly, has to face being deceived by false evidence involving clothes. God will not let him escape facing the consequences of his deeds. The punishment fits the crime.

Judah, attracted, offers to pay the disguised Tamar a goat for her services. She requests a pledge to guarantee that she will get the payment, and, very cleverly, she relieves him of three important bits of ancient ID: his signet, his cord, and his staff. As a result of this brief encounter she becomes pregnant. Judah is furious when he eventually hears about it and, not realizing that he is responsible, issues the chilling order: "Bring her out, and let her be burned" (Gen. 38:24). This is a horrific example of double standards. On the one hand, the man himself behaves like a Canaanite in using the services of what he thinks to be a cult prostitute and then, on the other hand, condemns his own daughter-in-law to death for behaving like one.

But she produces the pledged ID and has it presented to him: "By the man to whom these belong, I am pregnant. . . . Please identify whose these are, the signet and the cord and the staff" (38:25). These are the exact words that Judah and the others used when they took Joseph's coat to deceive Jacob. "Please identify . . ." God is getting through to Judah's conscience by applying the relentless principle, "With the measure you use it will be measured back to you." God does it because he loves the man, and "the Lord disciplines the one he loves" (Heb. 12:6).

Tamar's evidence is totally convincing. Judah is caught out and has no option but publicly to admit paternity. He also finds the courage to say that Tamar was more righteous than he, for he had failed in his duty toward her. In the midst of this sordid, moral mess, Judah begins to think of moral values. He is convicted of his sin. God has begun to work. Judah is beginning to learn. Yet it will take years to get him to true repentance.

This is an extreme situation, yes, but there is an important principle here. The issue is, how do we react when we are faced with incontrovertible evidence that we have done wrong? We get caught out in a lie. We are found responsible for spreading a very hurtful false rumor. We get caught speeding and try to get someone else to take the blame. How do we react to such situations?

Tamar gives birth to twins, the first of which is called Perez who will turn out to be an ancestor of King David and so an ancestor of the Messiah, Jesus Christ our Lord. What an astonishing story! At the end of his life Jacob says in his blessing of Judah, "The scepter shall not depart from Judah . . . until . . ." (Gen. 49:10). Perhaps that is a reference to the fact that it nearly did depart! Judah nearly lost his scepter in the literal sense by pledging it to a woman he thought to be a prostitute. The whole lineage of the Messiah, the whole Seed Project, was imperiled by Judah's behavior and hung on by just a thread, a very tenuous and messy thread.

Here, once more, we get a glimpse of the intricate way in which God's providence and human freedom interweave to generate actual history. From the human side Judah and Tamar are fully responsible for their actions, Judah driven by impulse and sexual lust and Tamar by desperation to be a mother. Yet above it all, God is King. He even uses Judah's sexual impropriety as a means of disciplining Judah for his deception of Jacob.

Later in Genesis we shall learn by profound contrast the way in which Joseph deals with sexual temptation. Now we must follow the Genesis narrative and get back to Joseph in Egypt. In order to bring some color into the picture, it is important to have some idea, however sketchy, of the land and culture of Egypt as it then was.

10

An Introduction to Egypt

Egypt's civilization is shaped by the Nile River, which is one of the longest rivers in the world. It flows northward through Africa, its drainage basin covering eleven countries, and issues into the Mediterranean Sea in a large delta. It is the primary water source for the Sudan and Egypt. Since ancient times it has been the lifeline for the country with most of the population and all of the cities situated on its banks north of Aswan. Indeed, only about two percent of the entire country is habitable. The Greek historian Herodotus wrote that "Egypt is the gift of the Nile."

The Importance of the Nile

The fertility of the Nile valley is sustained by an annual inundation when the river overflows its banks and deposits rich silt on the surrounding land. The importance of the river is seen by the fact that the ancient Egyptian calendar was based on three cycles, each consisting of four months of thirty days each: Akhet, the time of the inundation; Peret, the growing season; and Shemu, the harvest time, when there were no rains. The main crops were wheat and barley.

Archaeologist Kathryn Bard writes: "Essentially, during pharaonic times the Egyptians relied on the annual Nile flooding to water their fields. When the flooding was too low, less land could

be cultivated, which could create food shortages and possibly famine. When the flooding was too high, villages could be destroyed
and temples flooded. But with normal floods the potential for
cereal cultivation in this environment was enormous, and this
provided the economic base of the pharaonic state."[1]

The Bible gives us a description of what it would mean for
Egypt were the Nile to be dried up:

> Behold, the LORD is riding on a swift cloud
>   and comes to Egypt;
> and the idols of Egypt will tremble at his presence,
>   and the heart of the Egyptians will melt within them. . . .
>
> And the waters of the sea will be dried up,
>   and the river will be dry and parched,
> and its canals will become foul,
>   and the branches of Egypt's Nile will diminish and
>   dry up,
>   reeds and rushes will rot away.
> There will be bare places by the Nile,
>   on the brink of the Nile,
> and all that is sown by the Nile will be parched,
>   will be driven away, and will be no more.
> The fishermen will mourn and lament,
>   all who cast a hook in the Nile;
> and they will languish
>   who spread nets on the water.
> The workers in combed flax will be in despair,
>   and the weavers of white cotton.
> Those who are the pillars of the land will be crushed,
>   and all who work for pay will be grieved. (Isa. 19:1, 5–10)

Scholarly opinion tends to place Joseph's time in Egypt in
the Middle Kingdom (for a list of the major divisions of ancient

---

1. Kathryn Bard, *An Introduction to the Archaeology of Ancient Egypt*, 2nd ed. (Oxford, UK: Blackwell, 2015), 346.

Egyptian history, see the appendix). This was the epoch of Egypt's twelfth dynasty of eight pharaohs. The founder of the dynasty was Amenemhat I (1991–1962 BC). He elevated his son Sesostris I to be his coregent. Sesostris ruled from 1971–1928 BC and subdued northern Nubia. He was a prolific builder.

From the perspective of biblical chronology a crucial text is 1 Kings 6:1: "In the four hundred and eightieth year after the people of Israel came out of the land of Egypt, in the fourth year of Solomon's reign over Israel, in the month of Ziv, which is the second month, he began to build the house of the Lord." Scholarly opinion puts Solomon's fourth year as 966 BC. This puts the exodus around 1446 BC, which supports an early date for the exodus. Exodus 12:40–41 gives us further information: "The time that the people of Israel lived in Egypt was 430 years. At the end of 430 years, on that very day, all the hosts of the Lord went out from the land of Egypt."

Putting the two pieces of information together would mean that Jacob came to Egypt around 1876 BC. This would place Joseph at the time of the Middle Kingdom.

There are some other indications in Genesis that Joseph lived at this time. First, Joseph started his life in Egypt as a slave. Slavery did not exist in the Old Kingdom; the great pyramids were built by drafted peasant labor, not slave labor. The Middle Kingdom is the first major period in Egyptian history where slavery was well known. American Egyptologist William C. Hayes published a papyrus document from the Middle Kingdom that had a list of slaves and information about Egyptian prisons.[2]

The Hieratic Papyrus dating from the late twelfth dynasty to the thirteenth dynasty contains ninety-five entries of slave names, of which thirty can be identified as non-Egyptian. Several non-Egyptian names are either identical to or very similar to some names in the Old Testament. In this Papyrus published by Hayes,

---

2. See W. C. Hayes, ed., *A Papyrus of the Late Middle Kingdom in the Brooklyn Museum* (New York: Brooklyn Museum, 1972).

we have evidence that officials of wealth and standing also could own slaves. The Potiphar of Genesis must have been such a man.[3]

Second, we are told that just before Joseph went in for his first audience with Pharaoh, he shaved, indicating that Egyptians at the time did not approve of facial hair. The relevance of this is that in the later Hyksos period when Asiatic people ruled part of Egypt, this was not the case.

Literature

The language of the time was Middle Egyptian, a hieroglyphic (hiero = sacred, glyph = inscription) language comprising around nine hundred hieroglyphs. It was later amplified by the cursive hieratic script that was easier to write and so mainly employed for everyday writing, whereas the hieroglyphs were used for inscriptions on tombs and formal writing.

The glyphs have both semantic and phonetic values. For example, the glyph for *crocodile* is a picture of a crocodile that also represents the sound *msh*. When writing the word for *crocodile*, the ancient Egyptians combined a picture of a crocodile with the glyphs that spell out *msh*. Similarly the hieroglyphs for *cat, miw*, combine the glyphs for *m, i*, and *w* with a picture of a cat. The *Ancient History Encyclopedia* informs us:

> Ancient Egyptian literature comprises a wide array of narrative and poetic forms including inscriptions on tombs, stele, obelisks, and temples; myths, stories, and legends; religious writings; philosophical works; autobiographies; biographies; histories; poetry; hymns; personal essays; letters and court records. Although many of these forms are not usually defined as literature, they are given that designation in Egyptian studies because so many of them, especially

3. Charles Aling, "Joseph in Egypt, Part II," *Bible and Spade*, February 23, 2010, accessed November 7, 2018, http://www.biblearchaeology.org/post/2010/02/23/Joseph-in-Egypt-Part-II.aspx.

from the Middle Kingdom (2040–1782 BCE), are of such
high literary merit.[4]

The Gods of Egypt

Joseph's first seventeen years would have been filled with learning
from his father about the vision and the promise given to his great
grandfather Abraham. One can imagine he was thrilled with the
stories of God's providence and guidance, and, through listening
to them, had come to his own commitment to the one true Creator,
the God of Abraham, Isaac, and Jacob.

Now, like Daniel at a similar age, he found himself transplanted
in a polytheistic culture with a bewildering array of deities and a
vast collection of stories about them and their involvement with
the life and culture of Egypt. In order to understand what issues
Joseph faced in this connection, it will be useful for us to have
some idea of the considerable religious dimension to Egyptian life.
More than fifteen hundred names of Egyptian gods are on record,
perhaps the most famous of which are Amun the creator god and
Ra the sun God. Pharaoh was himself regarded as a god, Horus
the son of Ra. The list of gods is formidable. Following is more
about the two most prominent gods: Amun and Ra.

Amun

Initially, Amun was a local deity associated with Thebes. After
the pharaohs moved their capital to this city, worship of Amun
spread throughout the land of Egypt. Amun was the greatest of the
sun gods. During the eighteenth dynasty, the Egyptians combined
Amun with Ra, and he became the creative power behind all life.
He had two consorts, Amunet and Mut. Some of Amun's depictions show him as a man with a hawk's head and with a bull's tail
hanging from his tunic.

---

4. Johsua L. Mark, "Ancient Egyptian Literature," *Ancient History Encyclopedia*,
November 14, 2016, accessed September 12, 2018, https://www.ancient.eu/Egyptian
_Literature/.

Ra

Ra was a sun god, and some myths claimed that he created everything. He traveled through the sky in a boat, and he was the father and ruler of the gods. Depictions of Ra show him as a man with a hawk's head or as a hawk, but both types of images show him wearing a sun disc surrounded by an uraeus—a representation of a sacred serpent as an emblem of supreme power, worn on the headdresses of ancient Egyptian deities and sovereigns. The "son of Ra" was one of Pharaoh's titles. This title came from the belief that Ra would, at times, sleep with the queen to strengthen the bloodline of the pharaohs.

———

Although it is not relevant to our period, one of the fascinating facts about the history of Egyptian religion is that after the time of Joseph and of the exodus, from 1349–1333 BC, a period of only sixteen years, there was an unprecedented religious revolution under Amenhotep IV (who changed his name to Akhenaten), who abolished all the gods except one, Aten, the sun. He forced the population of Thebes, totaling over twenty thousand, to move to the new monotheistic cultic center at Amarna, abandoning their businesses, homes, and religion at Thebes. When Akhenaten died, there was a backlash against his enforced one-god religion, and his son Tutankh*aten* changed his name to Tutankh*amun*. Amarna was abandoned. The cult of Amun was soon revived. This episode is of great interest as one of the few incidences of henotheism in the ancient world.

In general, the ancient Egyptians believed that life arose from preexistent waters (the god Nun). The sun god Ra was self-created. An Egyptian text says: "He became, by himself." Ra then did two things. He brought order (ma'at) out of chaos by seizing control from eight preexistent gods, and he then called into being other gods, each of whom, like himself, personified a different part of nature. In turn they generated other gods and humans, the dividing line between them being obscure.

As for Ra, the sun god, Egyptians believed that he journeyed nightly into the underworld and then was reborn each day out of the waters of Nun. A symbolic expression of this was the fact that burials were carried out on the western side of the Nile and not the east. Human death did not mean the end of existence but traveling, like Ra, to the underworld. The dead were often buried with a "Book of the Dead," a document or collection of documents consisting of religious and magical texts that were designed to help their progression in the afterlife.

The Egyptian worldview was very different from that of Joseph. He believed in one eternal creator God who had created the universe and human life. The Egyptians believed in gods that were derived from the heavens, earth, and sea. In other words, the Egyptians had a theogony (an accounting of the origin of the gods), whereas Genesis has none. No one method of creation was universally accepted in ancient Egyptian literature.[5] The one that is of particular interest for students of the Bible is to be found on the Shabaka Stone, which attributes the formation of reality to the god Ptah: "The gods [of Ptah] are the teeth and lips from his mouth which proclaimed the name of everything." Carrid comments:

> Ptah is to be acclaimed as the omnipotent creator-god because he formed the cosmos by mere verbal fiat. He commanded with his teeth and lips, and the gods sprung forth. The description of Ptah's method of creation, otherwise known as the logos doctrine, should immediately remind us of the creative activity of Elohim in Genesis 1. That passage depicts God as creating the universe by the power of speech.[6]

A later passage on the Shabaka Stone says: "Indeed, all the divine order really came into being through what the heart thought and the tongue commanded."

---

5. John D. Currid, *Ancient Egypt and the Old Testament* (Grand Rapids, MI: Baker, 1997), 56.
6. Ibid., 61.

Indeed, the more one thinks about it, the more the Egyptian worldview resembled contemporary secular materialism, which, although it does not think explicitly in terms of "gods," it believes that the fundamental matter and forces of the universe have been responsible for "creating" everything else and therefore perform a godlike role. This means that Joseph's adult life was conducted against a very similar background to that of Daniel in Babylon.[7]

It is important to say that there is (as yet) no firm archaelogical evidence for Joseph's existence in Egypt, nor indeed for the exodus, although scholars are careful to point out that not only are records of the time scant, but Egyptians had a propensity for writing out of their history anything that showed them up in a bad light. An event of the nature and magnitude of the exodus would certainly have done that.

What we can say is that the information given in Genesis about the importance of the Nile, the dependence of Egypt on the grain harvest, and incidences of famine parallel what we know from other ancient sources and for that reason is credible.

---

7. John C. Lennox, *Against the Flow: The Inspiration of Daniel in an Age of Relativism* (Oxford, UK: Lion Hudson, 2015).

11

Joseph in the House of Potiphar

Joseph's first experience in Egypt was being bought as a household slave by a senior official, the captain of Pharaoh's guard, a man called Potiphar. As a senior military man he would have lived in a prominent building with a large retinue of servants and large estates to manage. Orientalist K. A. Kitchen writes:

> On the humblest level, we find in Papyrus Brooklyn 35.1446 among the forty-eight foreigners a variety of employments. Among the women were a variety of cloth makers, while the men were brewers, cooks, a children's guardian, and also *hery-per*, or domestic servants in the household. This last role was very common in Middle Kingdom Egypt, to judge from the large number of occurrences on family monuments.
>
> To begin with Joseph served "in the house" of his master (Gen. 39:2), obviously at the modest level, before being promoted (39:4–5) to be overseer of the house (hold). "In the house" he was a *hery-per*; after promotion he became an *imy-re per*, or steward. Over a large estate with subordinates of this title, one might become an *imy-re per wer*, or high steward. All these titles are very familiar in the Middle Kingdom, and the latter two also in the New Kingdom and later. But *hery-per* is

known especially from the Old and Middle Kingdoms (third
and early second millenia), not usually later.[1]

The phrase "the LORD was with Joseph" occurs several times
in the narrative at this juncture. He had lost his father and his
family. It is almost as if God compensates him for his loneliness
and isolation by allowing him to sense in a new way that he had
not abandoned him.

Yet how should we understand the phrase "the LORD was
with him" in the undesirable circumstance in which Joseph found
himself? It is so easy to write these words over our lives when
everything is going well, isn't it? But Joseph was Potiphar's slave.
He had no rights, and the future was decidedly bleak. Yet we are
emphatically told that the Lord was with him. We are to see the
providence of God behind what befalls Joseph. We must recognize
God's providence in our lives as well, because there are times when
we may find ourselves so weak and alone, when things aren't
going smoothly, that we imagine that the Lord has left us. Yet it
is not so.

The apostle Peter, when describing the sufferings of Christ and
the glories that should follow, mapped out for all Christians the
fact that they may often go through rough times *precisely* because
the Lord is with them. We would be superficial and naive to imagine that we're always going to have marvelous feelings and positive experiences, if we are Christians. Thank God when he gives
us good times. He often does, and that is wonderful. But if we
were to be guided solely by our feelings, we'd end up in spiritual
impoverishment. In Joseph we meet a man who was prepared to
reject some of the most powerful of human feelings because he had
subordinated them to the authority and will of God. One of the
evidences that the Lord was with Joseph was that the Lord gave
him *success* in everything he did. In fact, we are told that Potiphar
himself saw that the Lord was with Joseph!

---

1. K. A. Kitchen, *On the Reliability of the Old Testament* (Grand Rapids, MI: Eerdmans,
2006), 349.

Bearing in mind the polytheism of the culture, how did Potiphar see that the Lord was with Joseph? Presumably, it was at first the quality of his demeanor. The man was clearly not bitter. He was not harboring resentment against his brothers, even though his father had spoiled him when he was young. This high-powered military man, entrusted with the security of Pharaoh, saw something about Joseph that marked him out from others. All of that is very impressive, indeed, nothing less than amazing, considering Joseph's age.

I covet that, don't you? That people around us can see that we are different, that the Lord is with us, and they wish to know why. My mind immediately goes back many years to an encounter with a doctor who had given his life to Christian work. He came from a wealthy Jewish background and was building a promising career. Among his medical team was a nurse who was always cheerful whatever the pressure, never lost her temper or swore, and was constantly supportive. She was so different from the other medical staff he had to deal with—not that they were inadequate in any way, but there just was something about the nurse that intrigued him. One day he asked her outright, "What is so different about you?" She replied only one word: "Jesus." This made such an impression on him that he surreptitiously purchased a Bible and began to read it to find out about this Jesus, who meant so much to his nurse. Through reading it he became a believer in Christ. He subsequently lost his family and was rejected by them. Nevertheless, his faith grew, and he devoted his life to bringing health care and the Christian message to people far away from his original home. That nurse was like Joseph. God was with her, and the doctor saw it, and it brought a complete change of direction in his life.

Just as the nurse told the doctor what the secret of her life was, it is highly likely that Joseph did the same, telling Potiphar about the Lord when asked a similar question. Doubtless they had many an intelligent conversation as Joseph learned the language and customs of Egypt.

We do not always get to know what people learn from watching us. It is so important how we behave as Christians. We are to be different, as Jesus himself said; we are to be salt and light to the society around us.

What Potiphar sees generates trust and confidence in Joseph, and in the end Joseph is made the chief palace administrator or steward (*imy-re per wer*). This was a position carrying great responsibility. Stewards had an important role to play in the houses of prominent people in the ancient world. They were the ancient economists, responsible to see, as their name implies, that the the laws of the house were kept. The word *economist* comes from combining the Greek words *oikos* for "house" and *nomos* for "law."

It is likely that Joseph was also literate and in charge of whatever estates Potiphar owned. It would seem that at this time Egyptian economy was not money based, and people like Potiphar were rewarded for their services by being granted land and servants. Genesis tells us that God blessed Potiphar in house and field. Joseph's experience (admittedly not lengthy) with animals as a teenager would have come in handy. No doubt he had learned a lot from watching his brothers at work.

Joseph was a slave in status in a culture that did not assign much value to human life, but we should not think of his situation in terms of the awful form of slavery that was abolished by the tireless work of the Christian social activist William Wilberforce in the Slavery Abolition Act of 1833. Also, we should not forget that in the Greek and Roman world academics were all slaves (some of us are tempted to think we still are!). Earlier still in the Old Testament it is recorded that a slave could love his master, so much that he could say, "I don't want to go free. I want to serve you." That's very different from the kind of slavery that Wilberforce abolished and should not be confused with it. It is clear that throughout history, slavery took on various forms, some of them more humane than others.

However, we should also not forget the very disturbing fact
that there are still many slaves in the world today, men, women
and children suffering similar horrendous conditions of dehuman-
izing servitude similar to that which Wilberforce saw abolished
in England. Their numbers run into millions, and they are to be
found even in the most civilized of nations, where slave victims of
human trafficking are regularly discovered.

Joseph was a slave, but he clearly enjoyed considerable freedom as head steward of Potiphar's house. We can imagine that Potiphar was a fairly enlightened employer, prepared to trust people
when he saw evidence that they could be trusted. In contemporary
terms, Joseph became a high-powered administrator and manager
of a large organization.

Potiphar rapidly discovered that his confidence in Joseph was
well placed. His house was blessed (by the Lord, as we are told) at
every level so that Potiphar did not have to bother about anything
other than the food he ate (Gen. 39:6), a neat comment confirming
the authenticity of the Genesis document. Egyptians at the time
were like the French today: particular about their food.

Lessons from the Story

It will not have escaped our attention that Joseph's public witness took place in the workplace, and it raises the broader question of our own attitude as Christian believers to work and the
workplace.

We saw in our brief introduction to Genesis that work was
intended by the Creator to be an integral part of human life. God
assigned to the first humans the work of tending a garden. It was
an idyllic workplace where they enjoyed the immediate fellowship of God as they went about their activities. All that was but
distant history when Joseph entered his "employment" as steward
in Potiphar's palace. In the meantime, sin had entered the world
and brought with it damage to all levels of life. In particular, work
had become characterized by toil, indeed, for some it degenerated

into slave labor. The environment was no longer idyllic. Thorns and thistles both literal and metaphorical had sprung up. Think, for instance, of the unfairness of Joseph's situation. He was hated by his brothers and sold into slavery, yet he maintained a dignity, poise, and integrity that transcended the bitterness that would characterize many of us in his situation. The Lord was with him, we are told, and I am sure that Joseph himself sensed it. As a result his whole demeanor showed that he did his work not simply for Potiphar but ultimately for the Lord.

Joseph's approach to his work contains a vitally important principle that is emphasized for Christians in the New Testament. Paul writes: "Whatever you do, work heartily, as for the Lord and not for men, knowing that from the Lord you will receive the inheritance as your reward. You are serving the Lord Christ" (Col. 3:23–24). The operative word here is "whatever." The Lord is interested in every aspect of our lives, not simply in what we think of as our spiritual activities. Our daily work is to be done for him. He is interested in what we do at the workbench. His own Son was a carpenter.

This matter deserves further investigation since it is all too easy to fall into a compartmentalized way of living. Our time is carved up. Some time is given to God—personal devotions, going to church, and maybe some attention to Christian ministry. The main bulk of our time is given over to secular work. However, this falls very far short of the Christian work ethic. God is interested in the so-called secular part as well. He wishes us to develop a real sense that we can do our secular work as part of serving him.

If we were to ask the average person why he works, the answer is that he has a family to clothe and feed and a home to finance. If he is acquainted with the Bible, he may even justify this by quoting Paul's statement: "If anyone is not willing to work, let him not eat" (2 Thess. 3:10).

Incidentally, we should note carefully here what Paul does not say. He does not say, "If anyone *does* not work, neither let him eat." The difference is important. In countries with high unemployment, many people are very willing to work, but they cannot get a job. And this can affect them deeply. I recall one of my sons coming home from a job search and saying, "Nobody wants me, Dad." If God has given us work as part of what life means, then no wonder when people cannot find work, they often feel inadequate, unwanted, and unfulfilled, as my son did. Those of us who have employment ought therefore to be very thankful for it and ought never to look down on or, worse still, mock those who do not.

It is almost as if Paul foresaw the problem of unemployment. Of course, Paul was aware even then that there are lazy people who sponge on others and have no intention of working. He condemns them forthrightly in his very next statement: "We hear that some among you walk in idleness, not busy at work, but busybodies. Now such persons we command and encourage in the Lord Jesus Christ to do their work quietly and to earn their own living" (2 Thess. 3:11–12).

So far we have established that work is the norm for the Christian, and God has ordained it to be the usual source for our food and upkeep. Yet there is more to it than this, as we can see from a famous passage in the Sermon on the Mount, where Jesus addresses the topic of how we get the necessities of life. "No one can serve two masters," he says, "for either he will hate the one and love the other, or he will be devoted to the one and despise the other. You cannot serve God and money" (Matt. 6:24). Jesus clearly did not mean to say that we cannot serve God and *use* money. Indeed, there are many injunctions in the New Testament that are directed toward the wise use of money by those who serve God. To the rich Paul says:

> As for the rich in this present age, charge them not to be haughty, nor to set their hopes on the uncertainty of riches, but on God, who richly provides us with everything to enjoy. They are to do good, to be rich in good works, to be generous

and ready to share, thus storing up treasure for themselves as a good foundation for the future, so that they may take hold of that which is truly life. (1 Tim. 6:17–19)

Paul himself was grateful to those who supported him financially, Christians who had learned to serve God and use money in his service. The problem with the human heart is that it can so easily reverse this and try to serve money and use God as some kind of spiritual magician to get out of trouble.

Jesus continues in the Sermon on the Mount to explain what the correct attitude should be. He points to a major source of the tendency to make money the master of our lives—anxiety—and tells us to avoid it: "Therefore I tell you, do not be anxious about your life, what you will eat or what you will drink, nor about your body, what you will put on. Is not life more than food, and the body more than clothing?" (Matt. 6:25). How, then, are we to avoid anxiety?

Look at the birds of the air: they neither sow nor reap nor gather into barns, and yet your heavenly Father feeds them. Are you not of more value than they? And which of you by being anxious can add a single hour to his span of life? And why are you anxious about clothing? Consider the lilies of the field, how they grow: they neither toil nor spin, yet I tell you, even Solomon in all his glory was not arrayed like one of these. But if God so clothes the grass of the field, which today is alive and tomorrow is thrown into the oven, will he not much more clothe you, O you of little faith? Therefore do not be anxious, saying, 'What shall we eat?' or 'What shall we drink?' or 'What shall we wear?' For the Gentiles seek after all these things, and your heavenly Father knows that you need them all. But seek first the kingdom of God and his righteousness, and all these things will be added to you.

Therefore do not be anxious about tomorrow, for tomorrow will be anxious for itself. Sufficient for the day is its own trouble. (Matt. 6:26–34)

The argument is simple. It is our *heavenly Father* who provides food for birds and clothing for flowers. We, who are more valuable to him, are therefore to trust him for the necessities of life.

Anxiety and fear are real. Many years ago I was in Hungary and met a man whose demeanor impressed me greatly, a humble man of great grace and warmth. I was eager to hear his story. In the communist era he had been a village-school mathematics teacher, but he was also active in the local churches in the area, much in demand as a teacher of Scripture. One day he was summoned to the police station and questioned about his employment.

"You are a math teacher," they said, "but you are also a Bible teacher, is not that so?"

"Yes, indeed," he said, "I do that in my spare time."

"And you get paid for it?" they asked.

"Not at all," he said, "it is my contribution completely freely given."

"We do not believe you," they replied. "You must therefore choose. Either you continue as a school teacher or as a Bible teacher but not both, and you must give us your decision very soon."

He went home that night to his family with a heavy heart. He had a large family, and it was not easy to feed them all, yet he decided to discuss the matter with them. He called them together and said, "I never want you children to be able to say that they were not consulted by their father in big decisions affecting family life." So he outlined to them the choice he faced. What should he do?

The youngest boy in the family said, "Dad, I cannot imagine you without a Bible in your hands."

The decision was made and he had to leave the school. Finding work was difficult, and in the end he had to content himself with the backbreaking work of lifting and carrying heavy slates in a quarry. The slates had sharp edges, and his wife told me that many an evening she had to dress his hands with bandages so that the blood from his many abrasions would not drip onto the Bible he was using in the pulpit.

One day he was called into the manager's office. "I hear that you once taught mathematics?"

"That's right."

"Well," said the foreman, "I am underqualified for my job, and under new regulations we all need basic qualifications in mathematics. How would you like to teach me, instead of working in the quarry?" He jumped at it and discovered to his joy that his pay was more than he had received as a teacher in the school.

It was a magnificent example of what it means really to serve the Lord in daily work, and I was not surprised to discover that his influence was felt throughout the entire country.

There is, however, more to be thought about in Jesus's teaching in the Sermon on the Mount that we have just been considering. He speaks of motivation, contrasting two attitudes: "The Gentiles [pagans] seek. . . . [You] seek . . ." This strikes us as strange at first. Surely we are all to seek food and clothing by working, as God has ordained. That is true, of course, which means that it is not the point Jesus is making. Jesus is adding two further dimensions, the spiritual and the moral, to the quest for food and clothing, which is normally undertaken through our work. It is perhaps easiest understood when we think of it in the context of our motivation for doing that work.

One common motivation is simply to work in order to get money to live. On the other hand, Jesus says that the believer should "seek first the kingdom of God and his righteousness" in the process of gaining the wherewithal to live. The things necessary for living will be added as well, and here is the point—they are no longer the main motive for doing the work. For the believer, the main motive is to experience God's kingdom, that is, his rule in our everyday lives. In practical terms that will mean seeking his righteousness. Every job, every kind of work, whether paid or not, whether in a hospital, a factory, or a church, gives rise to moral problems, issues of personal and corporate probity.

Think of it this way: There are two aspects to work for a believer, not just one. First, the goal of work (as just mentioned): seeking God's rule; and then the by-products of work: food, clothing, housing, etc. The sad tragedy is that many people confuse the goal of work with the by-product of work. For them the main goal of work is food, clothing, housing, and all the rest of an inexhaustible list of private possessions, up to private aircraft, yachts, palaces, and even football clubs. Their prime motivation is to get these things. The danger is that their desire to possess them may overrule moral qualms, and they may give in to the temptation to acquire them by dishonesty, cheating, corruption, theft, and a thousand other different ways of manipulating the system.

What such people do not realize is that although they may well have gained goods and property, they have lost the main objective for which work was intended by God in the first place—experiencing his rule and righteousness. God is interested in character far more than possessions. His intention is that our work becomes an integral part of the process of character development.

My Hungarian friend exemplified this memorably. Another vivid example I came across is that of a young man in his twenties who had trained as an electrician. After just a few weeks in his first job doing the electrical wiring in new houses, he was summoned to see his boss, who angrily accused him of laziness in that he had wired fewer houses than his workmates. He replied that he could not work any faster, since the wiring under the floors had to be done especially carefully to fulfill the regulations regarding fire hazards. The boss angrily retorted: "Who sees under the floorboards?"

"My Lord does," answered the young man without hesitation. He was fired on the spot but got a new job soon afterward.

This incident captures exactly what Jesus teaches. The young electrician was seeking God's rule and righteousness in his daily work. He was not prepared to cut moral corners because he believed God was interested in his character. God was watching the way he worked.

12

Joseph and Potiphar's Wife

The very first temptation happened in the garden in Eden, the garden which the first humans were given the responsibility of tending. This was the workplace of Adam and Eve.

Joseph also experienced temptation in the workplace, Potiphar's palace. There was a woman in the palace, Potiphar's wife. One can imagine her as beautiful, rich, and bored. She imagined she could risk having some fun with this handsome steward, for Joseph was good-looking, as his mother had been. Or is that being unfair to Potiphar's wife? May it not have been that she, given ample opportunity to see Joseph at work, gradually fell in love with him? Not surprisingly, opinions differ, and both scenarios are realistic.

Joseph certainly could not avoid noticing Potiphar's wife. Indeed, many people today might well have said, "Joseph, indulge yourself. Have your fun, man, if you get the chance! No one is going to see you. What harm is there in it? She is very beautiful, and available, and you are lonely and have nothing to lose."

Furthermore, in that ancient society, if Joseph had done so, it could well have been a way of taking over from Potiphar and so gaining real power and status. So the stakes were high, as eventually she cajoled him and tried to get him to sleep with her. It was a powerful temptation at the workplace. It faces many men today. How many married men work with an attractive young secretary, twenty years their junior? Before long the older partner is replaced by a younger model, the marriage disintegrates, and the children suffer the most.

Joseph was not married at this time but was a normal young man with normal, healthy, God-given desires, and surely he would have been delighted to have a wife, as he eventually did. How would he handle his natural desires and his awareness of his own desirability?

God is not against sex; after all, he invented it as a wonderful aspect of human life, essential to procreation. But God is against adultery, that destroyer of marriage and families. And Joseph was seeking God's rule in his life and was not prepared to take some-one's else's wife. We should listen carefully to what he says to Potiphar's wife as he resists her advances:

> Behold, because of me my master has no concern about any-thing in the house, and he has put everything that he has in my charge. He is not greater in this house than I am, nor has he kept back anything from me except you, because you are his wife. (Gen. 39:8–9)

Some interpretations of this event do not deal kindly with Joseph. For instance, Maurice Samuel writes:

> Does he [Joseph] have to emphasize the fact that he could as-suage her need safely if he wanted to? "He knoweth not what is in the house." Does Joseph have to point out that he is the equal of her husband? . . . In reality it was Joseph who forced the issue, as he had done in his boyhood with his brothers, forced it steadily day by day, until the explosion came. In those days he had played with his brothers' hatred; now he toyed with a woman's love. In both instances he was the active agent, and set the pattern; and to make this clear, in both instances

he had his coat torn off him—in a kind of unmasking—and was thrown into the pit.[1]

Plausible as this suggestion may appear from a certain perspective, I do not myself find it convincing for the following reason. The narrative at this point concerns a situation in which everything is permitted, with one exception. We have read something very like that before—the story of the original temptation in Genesis 3. The resonances are strong: not now a beautiful garden, but a beautiful palace; not Eve but another woman appealing to aesthetic and basic human drives; not now to eat a forbidden fruit but to taste the forbidden fruit that she herself was. Thomas Mann recognizes this allusion when he has Joseph say to her, "Understand me rightly—I dare not take a bite of the lovely apple you offer me, that we may eat of wrongdoing and ruin everything."[2]

Yet what a world of difference there was between the situation in the garden and the one in Potiphar's house. Adam, perfectly created from the hand of God, with his eyes wide open, took his eye off the spiritual and moral dimension and fell for the temptation offered by his wife, thereby bringing disaster to the world. Eating the tree promised the knowledge of good and evil, a knowledge that proved Adam's undoing. But Joseph, maybe in his early twenties by this time, shows that his knowledge of good and evil is very different from that of Adam. It led him to refuse the evil. "How then can I do this great wickedness and sin against God?" (Gen. 39:9). Joseph's reply to her shows that his ethics were not of the situational variety that characterizes much relativistic thinking: "If it feels right, it must be right." For Joseph there were absolute values; there was such a thing as sin.

He regarded the particular sin tempting him not only to be against Potiphar but ultimately against God, who had defined marriage as an exclusive bond between a man and a woman until

1. Maurice Samuel, *Certain People of the Book* (New York: Knopf, 1959), 330.
2. Thomas Mann, *Joseph and His Brothers: The Stories of Jacob, Young Joseph, Joseph in Egypt, Joseph the Provider*, trans. John E. Woods (New York: Knopf, 2005), 949.

one of them dies. She was Potiphar's wife, and Joseph saw that giving in to her desires would be an offense not only against Potiphar but also against God. The sad irony here is that Joseph valued Potiphar's trust; his wife did not.

How different Joseph was from his half-brother Judah, to whose sexual behavior Genesis drew our attention a short while ago.

There is a clear message here for our contemporary world. Where early sexual activity, including pornography, is encouraged, in the words of a former British chief rabbi Immanuel Jakobovitz, it leads to a "moral wasteland." The cost, he says, to society of marital infidelity is incalculable, above all in terms of the millions of children being raised in a moral wasteland, without the shelter of a loving home. Is it any wonder that from their number countless embittered, selfish, lonely and sometimes violent citizens, are recruited to swell the ranks of the anti-social?

The only way of dealing with this kind of powerful temptation of lust is to make God the center and focal point of our morality, not our desires, or feeling that it is so right.

Potiphar's wife did not relent. Joseph must have had an increasingly difficult time resisting as she kept the pressure up day after day. Many a man has resisted once but given in when the pressure persists. Joseph did not, dealing with it by avoiding her. Finally, at a time when the house was empty, in desperation, she seized his cloak and pulled him to her. His only means of escape was to run, which meant leaving his robe in her hands. His first robe had been forcibly taken off him by his hate-inspired brothers; his second, by a lust-driven woman. Joseph lost his robe but retained his integrity.

Centuries later Paul would give similar advice to young Christians: "Flee youthful passions" (2 Tim. 2:22). There are some pressures you can escape only by literally running out of the situation. Joseph's doing so represents a crucial stage in the ongoing biblical storyline, for this is a book in which, in the interests of the Seed

Project, a great deal of attention is given to the question of who marries whom. Joseph will not sleep with another man's wife.

Her thwarted passion led to boundless fury, "a woman scorned." First, she denounced Joseph to the other servants, playing the race card:

> As soon as she saw that he had left his garment in her hand and had fled out of the house, she called to the men of her household and said to them, "See, he has brought among us a Hebrew to laugh at us. He came in to me to lie with me, and I cried out with a loud voice. And as soon as he heard that I lifted up my voice and cried out, he left his garment beside me and fled and got out of the house. (Gen. 39:13–15)

This accusation opens a window into her character, for she blames her husband to the servants, a very serious and unwise breach of etiquette in that culture, to say the least.

> Then she laid up his garment by her until his master came home, and she told him the same story, saying, "The Hebrew servant, whom you have brought among us, came in to me to laugh at me. But as soon as I lifted up my voice and cried, he left his garment beside me and fled out of the house." (39:16–18)

To Potiphar she says that Joseph came in to mock her, adding, no doubt with relish: "This is the way your servant treated me" (v. 19). It is possible, though, that her reference to mocking has the sense of "play," including sexual play. She instantly changes from the aggressor to the victim, loud in her protest against the "outrage." What she does is increasingly relevant to developments in the very different culture of contemporary Western society.

According to Bradley Campbell and Jason Manning, this is the rise of the so-called "culture of victimhood in which individuals and groups display high sensitivity to slight, have a tendency to handle conflicts through complaints to third parties, and seek to cultivate an image of being victims who deserve assistance."[3] Bradley and Manning contrast contemporary victim culture with earlier honor and dignity cultures, the categories of which are far more likely to describe the Egypt of Joseph's time, which is why Potiphar's wife's behavior is so striking. Of course, there are situations in which people are real victims and need to experience justice, but that is not the case here.

Potiphar, we are told, responded angrily, though perhaps the text carefully avoids saying with whom he was angry. He ordered Joseph to be incarcerated in the special prison reserved for the king's prisoners. So far as we know, there were very few prisons in the ancient world, but, as we saw in connection with the evidence for slavery in the Middle Kingdom, there are records of prisons in Egypt.

The fact that Potiphar did not have Joseph executed, the usual punishment for adultery, may indicate that he had suspicions about the veracity of his wife's story and wished to give Joseph, who had been a huge asset to him, some benefit of the doubt. Potiphar probably had no option but to keep such suspicions to himself in order to avoid his own status being threatened by scandal. After all, there were no other witnesses; the house was empty.

This fact has led some commentators to put part of the blame on Joseph for acting unwisely in going into an empty building with a woman who had been constantly pestering him. Of course, he may not have known it was empty. It probably was a large house, and she may well have chosen her moment carefully. Whatever happened, there is an obvious warning for us today: people should avoid finding themselves alone with people of the opposite sex in situations where they could easily compromise in unforeseen ways.

This is now the third time in the story of Joseph that clothes have been used as false evidence. First was the use of Joseph's blood-

---

3. Bradley Campbell and Jason Manning, *The Rise of Victimhood Culture: Microaggressions, Safe Spaces, and the New Culture Wars* (New York: Palgrave Macmillan, 2018), 11.

stained cloak to deceive Jacob into thinking Joseph was dead; next was Tamar's clothing herself as a prostitute in order to deceive her father-in-law, Judah; and once more in a sexual context, Potiphar's wife uses Joseph's cloak to frame her husband. Joseph's first cloak was a garment of distinction, and so presumably was this second one, as befitted a chief steward in the home of one of the elite.

Joseph had done the right thing. Potiphar's wife had committed the crime, but Joseph was suffering for it. The apostle Peter warns that this kind of suffering is likely to happen to Christian believers:

> If when you do good and suffer for it you endure, this is a gracious thing in the sight of God. For to this you have been called, because Christ also suffered for you, leaving you an example, so that you might follow in his steps. He committed no sin, neither was deceit found in his mouth. When he was reviled, he did not revile in return; when he suffered, he did not threaten, but continued entrusting himself to him who judges justly. (1 Pet. 2:20–23)

The supreme example of someone who suffered for doing right and good is the Lord Jesus himself. The remarkable thing is that Joseph, who knew nothing of Jesus, behaved like him.

To be accused of something you did not do is a terrible experience, especially if, as was the case with Joseph, in the area of sexual misdemeanor or child abuse. Yet such accusations are on the increase in our society. This has given rise to a new category of person, the falsely accused. In many countries there are Christians today sitting in prisons falsely accused of crimes they never committed.

There is no indication in the text that Joseph was given any opportunity to explain his side of the story, which is often the case in such situations. When we are wrongly and deceitfully accused, the immediate temptation is to protest and lash out, which is why Peter draws the example of Jesus to our attention. When Jesus was falsely accused and abominably treated, he did not lash out, he did not return the insults, he did not threaten. What he did do is of paramount importance. He kept quiet and entrusted himself to God the righteous judge.

Similarly Paul advises his fellow believers: "Beloved, never avenge yourselves, but leave it to the wrath of God, for it is written, 'Vengeance is mine, I will repay, says the Lord'" (Rom. 12:19). This is not easy advice to take. When we are falsely accused, or even when we are cheated of something that we think should rightfully have been ours (think of the problems arising from legacies even in your own wider family circle), it can be a hard struggle to get to the stage where we are prepared to let it go and entrust it to God in the confidence that he will deal with it fairly and justly in the end.

Also increasingly problematic in contemporary society, particularly in our colleges and universities, is the occurrence of microaggression that we referred to earlier. What frequently happens here is that what used to be thought of as a minor grievance—e.g., a verbal insult or a politically incorrect statement—that could be resolved between those immediately involved, is instead blown out of all proportion by means of an official complaint to some institutional authority and/or is spread far and wide on social media. In each case a third party is called in. In addition, the complainant seeks for further small incidents and adds them together to make a case that the matter in hand is much more serious than perhaps a single issue would indicate.

Campbell and Manning write:

Other strategies for swaying third parties have the same core logic: they increase intervention by magnifying the actual or apparent severity of the conflict. While some aggrieved individuals increase the apparent severity by documenting a larger pattern of offense, in other cases the manipulation of information is more extreme: Not content merely to publicize the offensive behavior of their adversaries, the aggrieved might exaggerate its extent or even make it up whole cloth. In interpersonal disputes someone might make a false accusation against an adversary, as when a woman who is spurned by a man falsely accuses him of rape or when someone falsely accuses an ex-spouse of child abuse.[4]

They might well be describing Potiphar's wife.

I mention this issue because Christians have to be aware of such dangers and be careful not to precipitate accusations of microaggression. They also need to be careful to avoid being infected by our culture, since the concept of dealing with every little complaint by appealing to third parties and proclaiming your victimhood is not the way taught by Jesus and his apostles. Rather, if we have a complaint against someone, we should try to sort it out privately, and only if that fails should we get another person involved, and only if that fails should we go to the church (not the world) and seek help. The basic principle is containment, the exact opposite of the public broadcasting of accusations of microaggression.

On the other hand, as we are only too keenly aware in the current "Me Too" climate in some countries, there are many real victims of sexual assault for which the principle of containment does not apply, and the authorities need to be alerted in order to prosecute the perpetrators and prevent them destroying further lives.

We cannot leave this episode in Joseph's life without thinking about the question of what happens if we fail to do what Joseph did, and we fall into temptation, which realism and experience tell us can happen. The Bible does not comment on this here in Genesis but has a great deal to say about it elsewhere. What comes to mind at once is the behavior of Israel's greatest king, David, who saw from his palace roof a beautiful woman and summoned her to the palace, where he slept with her. But Bathsheba was another man's wife, and when she became pregnant, David eventually arranged for her husband, Uriah, to be killed in battle.

---

4. Ibid.

Guilty of adultery, deceit, and murder, David was the polar opposite of Joseph. Yet God did not destroy David but sent the prophet Nathan to confront him with the devastating consequences of what he had done:

> Now therefore the sword shall never depart from your house, because you have despised me and have taken the wife of Uriah the Hittite to be your wife. Thus says the LORD, "Behold, I will raise up evil against you out of your own house. And I will take your wives before your eyes and give them to your neighbor, and he shall lie with your wives in the sight of this sun. For you did it secretly, but I will do this thing before all Israel and before the sun." (2 Sam. 12:10–12)

Faced with this, David at once confessed his guilt: "David said to Nathan, 'I have sinned against the LORD'" (12:13a). And Nathan said to David, "The LORD also has put away your sin; you shall not die. Nevertheless, because by this deed you have utterly scorned the LORD, the child who is born to you shall die" (12:13b–14).

There are two major lessons to be learned from this. The first is that God is rich in forgiveness for those who repent. David might have written Psalm 32 to express his experience of God's mercy at the time:

> Blessed is the one whose transgression is forgiven,
>   whose sin is covered.
> Blessed is the man against whom the LORD counts no
>   iniquity,
>   and in whose spirit there is no deceit. (vv. 1–2)

God forgave David, but (and this is the second lesson) sin has consequences. In David's case those consequences were irreversible and wrought havoc on his family for many years.

It is a serious mistake to think that forgiveness removes the consequences of sin. If I get drunk behind the wheel of a car and knock you down and injure your spine, leaving you paraplegic, maybe after some time, with God's grace and my repentance, you might be prepared to forgive me. You will, however, still be paraplegic. The Christian who sins is called upon to repent with the promise, "If we confess our sins, he is faithful and just to forgive us our sins and to cleanse us from all unrighteousness" (1 John 1:9). The consequences are another matter. They have to be lived with. Forgiveness does not cancel them. It is important that we realize this.

The topic of forgiveness will figure prominently in the Joseph narrative later. It will, however, not be a question of Joseph seeking forgiveness but of Joseph doing the forgiving.

In the meantime we should get back to where we left him in his prison cell in Egypt.

13

Joseph in Prison

The first thing we read about Joseph in the prison is this:

> The LORD was with Joseph and showed him steadfast love and
> gave him favor in the sight of the keeper of the prison. And the
> keeper of the prison put Joseph in charge of all the prisoners who
> were in the prison. Whatever was done there, he was the one who
> did it. The keeper of the prison paid no attention to anything that
> was in Joseph's charge, because the LORD was with him. And
> whatever he did, the LORD made it succeed. (Gen. 39:21–23)

Joseph had proved a trustworthy administrator in Potiphar's
house. He now proves himself to be an equally trustworthy administrator in the prison. We are told that the Lord was with him,
and we see at once that we may not interpret the Lord's being with
him as a guarantee that life would go swimmingly. Joseph was in
prison, and the Lord was with him. That did not mean immediate or even rapid release. What it did mean was that God had not
forgotten him and was still involved in his life. Joseph was part
of a much bigger story than he could possibly have imagined or
appreciated at this stage. His prison experience was a necessary
part of his training to fulfill a central role in God's purposes for
his people and for the world at large.

Joseph's administrative skills were soon noticed inside the prison. Whatever his reaction to his unfair imprisonment, it did not prevent him from actively making the best of his situation. He did this with such success that he was eventually placed in charge of running the prison, a surprising position for an inmate to be given. One cannot help wondering if the prison governor may have begun to suspect that Joseph had been imprisoned on a false charge.

The next significant thing to happen in the drama was the arrival in the prison of two special prisoners from Pharaoh's entourage: the cupbearer and the baker. They had offended their master. Responsible for the king's food and drink, such men were often suspects in plots to poison the king. Whatever the charge against them, they were placed in custody in the house of the captain of the guard, in the same prison where Joseph was confined. The captain of the guard assigned Joseph to attend them personally, probably with instructions to observe them carefully and find out exactly what they were guilty of so this could be reported to Pharaoh.

One day Joseph noticed that the cupbearer and the baker seemed dejected and out of sorts and he asked them why.

"We have had dreams," they answered, "and there is no one to interpret them."

Then Joseph said to them, "Do not interpretations belong to God? Please tell them to me" (Gen. 40:8).

So the chief cupbearer told Joseph his dream:

> In my dream there was a vine before me, and on the vine there were three branches. As soon as it budded, its blossoms shot forth, and the clusters ripened into grapes. Pharaoh's cup was in my hand, and I took the grapes and pressed them into Pharaoh's cup and placed the cup in Pharaoh's hand. (40:9–11)

Joseph replied:

> This is its interpretation: the three branches are three days. In three days Pharaoh will lift up your head and restore you to

your office, and you shall place Pharaoh's cup in his hand as formerly, when you were his cupbearer. Only remember me, when it is well with you, and please do me the kindness to mention me to Pharaoh, and so get me out of this house. For I was indeed stolen out of the land of the Hebrews, and here also I have done nothing that they should put me into the pit. (40:12–15)

Before we look at the details, it is worth noting that the imagery bears a hallmark of authenticity. The cupbearer is said to squeeze grapes into Pharaoh's cup. This refers to the fact that one of the cupbearer's responsibilities was to ensure that the king did not disgrace himself by drinking too much alcohol on important occasions. The cupbearer would do this by surreptitiously diluting the wine with grape juice.

Joseph noticed that they were sad. That says something impressive about his state of mind. One can easily imagine that many of us, if we had been as badly treated as Joseph, might well have given in to the destructive emotions of self-pity, bitterness, and anger because of our own situation, and we would never have noticed something as marginal as the sad faces of a couple of prisoners. Do we notice the emotional state of those around us? One of our basic human needs is to be noticed, and people know if we are really interested in them or if our interaction with them is superficial and perfunctory.

Joseph had, apparently, managed to rise so far above his own circumstances that he was aware—indeed, compassionately aware—of what was going on in the lives of those around him. This represents a challenge to us who may well enjoy much more favorable circumstances than he did at that time. He noticed, and he asked what was wrong, and they told him about their dreams and their desire to have them interpreted.

Years before, Joseph himself had dreamed, and so far his dreams had come to nothing. He might well have told the cupbearer and the baker to forget their dreams, that there was no more substance in them than in his own dreams. Yet he didn't. On the contrary, he said: "Do not interpretations belong to God? Please tell them to me."

I wonder what they thought he meant by "God." In the narrative Joseph tells the two men that he had been "stolen out of the land of the Hebrews" (40:15), so at some stage in the conversation, he may well have explained to them about the God of the Hebrews.

Whatever the answer to that question, one thing is clear: Joseph had not given up on his own dreams. His mention of God in connection with dreams surely indicates that he still had a deep confidence that God was behind the dreams he had had and would eventually bring them to fulfillment. One can imagine that he understood his dreams as promises from God on which he could rely, however little he understood them. What is striking is that although Joseph does not appear to have understood his own dreams, he still is confident that he can interpret the dreams of the two prisoners.

Joseph did not have the Bible. So far as we know from Genesis, he did not even have the experience his forefathers did of God speaking directly. But he did know that God had spoken in his dream, and that fact gave him an inward stability and an outward-looking attitude, so he could notice when those around him were in trouble.

We do have the Bible, yet it is possible that our enthusiasm for believing its promises to us has diminished over the years. Some of us, when we first trusted the Lord years ago, were filled with a sense of joy while reading Scripture, as we heard the Lord speak through it. And now? If our interest in the Word of God were judged by the amount of time we spend reading it, what would it look like? We've stopped believing, have we? It is even possible for those of us involved in Christian ministry to spend proportionately little time listening to God speaking through his Word.

Joseph interpreted the dreams of the two prisoners. He explained to them that the number three that appears in each of their dreams represented a time interval. Specifically, he told the chief cupbearer that the three branches he had seen meant that he would be restored to his position within three days, and Joseph asked him to mention to Pharaoh the unjust treatment Joseph had experienced. Joseph told the chief baker that the three baskets of cakes in his dream portended his execution within three days.

Three days later both dreams were fulfilled on Pharaoh's birthday. The baker was executed, and the cupbearer got his job back. But he forgot Joseph.

Joseph certainly did not forget him. His hopes of release must have been high when he asked the cupbearer to mention him favorably to Pharaoh. But when nothing happened the next day or the next week or month or year, he must have become increasingly disappointed. How could the cupbearer have forgotten Joseph's role in giving him hope? Was Joseph wrong in thinking that God was providentially behind his meeting with the cupbearer under such circumstances? Or, as some think, was Joseph wrong in trying to do something in his own defense, to get himself a hearing, rather than simply remaining quiet and allowing God to act? I think that is too harsh of a judgment. Joseph may understandably have thought that the cupbearer could be a conduit to a fair hearing and freedom.

All that had happened to him was unfair and unjust. He had done nothing to deserve being in Egypt, let alone being in an Egyptian prison. Potiphar should have sensed that Joseph had protected rather than insulted him. The silence of God became intense for Joseph. It must have been increasingly hard to take. The question asked in the Psalms must have been his constant companion: "How long, O Lord?" Maybe, though, he clung to the fact that since the dreams of the cupbearer and the baker had come true, so also would his own.

Turning Point: Pharaoh's Dreams

Two long years went by with no change in Joseph's situation. Then one night Pharaoh dreamed a double dream that disturbed him deeply. From the time of the Middle Kingdom (2000 BC onward) there was a great deal of Egyptian literature concerning dreams. John Currid tells us that kings often claimed to receive commands from deities in dreams, and, in general, dreams were regarded as important vehicles for conveying the will of the gods. According to Currid:

> The most important collection of dream omens is the Chester Beatty Papyrus III which comes from Dynasty 19. Alan Gardiner maintains that the style and language of the document may be dated as early as Dynasty 12 (ca. 1991–1783 BC). . . . The manuscript is divided into dreams experienced by the Sons of Seth and the Sons of Horus. Over columns listing various dreams are written the words,

> "If a man sees himself in a dream:
>   Seeing a large cat—Good: it means a large harvest will come to him.
>   Seeing his face in a mirror—Bad: it means another wife."[1]

Another example from the same period is that if a man saw himself submerged in the Nile, that was a good omen, symbolizing that he had been purified of all evil. But seeing a dwarf in a dream portended the tragedy of having his life cut in half.[2]

> Pharaoh dreamed that he was standing by the Nile, and behold, there came up out of the Nile seven cows, attractive and plump, and they fed in the reed grass. And behold, seven other cows, ugly and thin, came up out of the Nile after them, and stood by the other cows on the bank of the Nile. And the ugly, thin cows ate up the seven attractive, plump cows. And Pharaoh awoke. And he fell asleep and dreamed a second time. And behold, seven ears of grain, plump and

---

1. John D. Currid, *Ancient Egypt and the Old Testament* (Grand Rapids, MI: Baker, 1997), 225–26.
2. *Archaeological Study Bible*, ed. Walter Kaiser Jr. and Duane Garrett (Grand Rapids, MI: Zondervan, 2005), 741.

good, were growing on one stalk. And behold, after them sprouted seven ears, thin and blighted by the east wind. And the thin ears swallowed up the seven plump, full ears. And Pharaoh awoke, and behold, it was a dream. So in the morning his spirit was troubled, and he sent and called for all the magicians of Egypt and all its wise men. Pharaoh told them his dreams, but there was none who could interpret them to Pharaoh. (Gen. 41:1–8)

Among those who heard about Pharaoh's concern about his dreams was the chief cupbearer, whose memory was prompted. He reminded Pharaoh of his brief spell in prison, described the dreams he had had, and told Pharaoh about the "young Hebrew" (41:12) who had been able to interpret them accurately.

Pharaoh lost no time in summoning Joseph, who had a shave,[3] changed his clothes, and went in to the king. Joseph's life is about to change dramatically. However, we should not move on before we have thought of the significance, not of Pharaoh's dreams but of when they occurred. For, as will soon be made clear by Joseph, the dreams were sent by God, who was therefore responsible for their timing.

That means that God was directly responsible for the two long years that Joseph had to wait from the time the cupbearer was reinstated. Furthermore, it is clear that God could have prompted the cupbearer much earlier to put in a word for Joseph with Pharaoh. That might have brought Joseph's freedom, but it certainly would not have taken him to a position of great influence. Joseph's capacity to interpret Pharaoh's dreams would play the central role. But the thought recurs: God could have sent Pharaoh the dreams earlier. He did not. Why?

Perhaps the answer lies in the terse reference to Joseph in Psalm 105:19: "The word of the LORD tested him." Joseph's integrity had certainly been tested in the encounter with Potiphar's wife.

---

3. Another mark of authenticity—apparently, unlike other ancient peoples, Egyptians at the time shaved.

Could it be that he was being tested in a different way by having to wait? Admittedly, waiting is a totally alien idea to a generation taught to expect instant gratification. Yet waiting on the Lord is a thoroughly biblical notion:

> They who wait for the LORD shall renew their strength;
>> they shall mount up with wings like eagles;
> they shall run and not be weary;
>> they shall walk and not faint. (Isa. 40:31)

It is a thought that we meet in the Psalms:

> I waited patiently for the LORD;
>> he inclined to me and heard my cry. (Ps. 40:1)

> Wait for the LORD;
>> be strong, and let your heart take courage;
> wait for the LORD! (Ps. 27:14)

Waiting is hardest when you are suffering, and many of the psalms express that in prayer: "How long, O Lord?" Many of the major characters in Scripture had to wait, sometimes an inordinately long time, to see the fulfillment of the promises that God had made to them. Apart from Joseph, Abraham, Moses, and David spring immediately to mind.

What is clear from experience is that waiting builds character. Those people who had to save hard in earlier life and wait to afford to get married, have a home, get labor-saving devices such as washing machines, purchase new clothes, and eat at restaurants—tend to have a different sense of appreciation for what they have compared with those who got everything they wanted instantly.

In 2013 the *Huffington Post* reported:

> In a world of instant gratification, it can seem like the concept of "waiting" is on the verge of extinction. But learning to wait builds character and could even improve decision-making skills, a new study suggests. Researchers from the University of

Chicago Booth School of Business found that the act of waiting increases patience, and that patience seems to help people
make smarter decisions about money. "When people wait,
it makes them place a higher value on what they're waiting
for, and that higher value makes them more patient," study
researcher Ayelet Fishbach said in a statement. "They see more
value in what they are waiting for because of a process psy-
chologists call self-perception—we learn what we want and
prefer by assessing our own behavior, much the same way we
learn about others by observing how they behave."[4]

In the Christian context Paul makes the point in Romans 5:1–5:

> Therefore, since we have been justified by faith, we have peace
> with God through our Lord Jesus Christ. Through him we
> have also obtained access by faith into this grace in which we
> stand, and we rejoice in hope of the glory of God. Not only
> that, but we rejoice in our sufferings, knowing that suffering
> produces endurance, and endurance produces character, and
> character produces hope, and hope does not put us to shame,
> because God's love has been poured into our hearts through
> the Holy Spirit who has been given to us.

The glory of God is yet future for the believer, and suffering may
come before then. Even there, says Paul, we can be confident (the
meaning of "rejoice") because we know that endurance produces
character that generates a hope that will not let us down. This was
no armchair thinking for Paul:

> For we do not want you to be unaware, brothers, of the afflic-
> tion we experienced in Asia. For we were so utterly burdened
> beyond our strength that we despaired of life itself. Indeed, we

4. "Waiting Builds Patience—and Leads to Smarter Decision-Making," October 7, 2013, *Huffington Post* website, accessed December 31, 2018, e-healthynewsdaily.blogspot.com/2013 /10/waiting-builds-patience-and-leads-to.html. The study was published in Xianchi Dai and Ayelet Fishbach, "When Waiting to Choose Increases Patience," *Journal of Organizational Behavior and Human Decision Processes*, vol. 121 (July 2013): 256–66.

felt that we had received the sentence of death. But that was to
make us rely not on ourselves but on God who raises the dead.
He delivered us from such a deadly peril, and he will deliver
us. On him we have set our hope that he will deliver us again.
(2 Cor. 1:8–10)

It takes real character to distinguish between God's no and his
not yet.

There is a clear connection between endurance and character
and reliance on God that we may legitimately read back into the
life of Joseph. The long wait in prison contributed to the depth
of character he would need to cope with high administrative responsibility, to say nothing of the resources he would need for the
process of being reconciled to his brothers.

14

Joseph's Rise to Power

The long wait is over, and Joseph, now thirty years old, stands before the most powerful monarch on earth at the time, the leader of the Egyptian superpower. Joseph surely sensed that something was about to happen that would make sense of his own dreams.

"I have had a dream," said Pharaoh, "and there is no one who can interpret it. I have heard it said of you that when you hear a dream you can interpret it" (Gen. 41:15). Joseph's reply is magnificent: "It is not in me; God will give Pharaoh a favorable answer" (41:16).

Joseph did not claim to be an interpreter of dreams. He claimed to know the God who had sent them and would explain them to him. What, then, did the polytheistic king understand by Joseph's use of the word *God*? Initially, probably very little, except for the obvious and important fact that this God was unknown in Egypt.

No god of Egypt could enable humans to interpret dreams. That was clear from the fact that Pharaoh had a retinue of wise men, magicians, and astrologers to guide him. They professed contact with the gods, but when it came to it, they had none. Pharaoh told his experts the content of the dream, but they proferred no explanation, for fairly obvious reasons arising out of the content of the dreams.

Pharaoh's dreams concerned the river Nile, which was central to Egyptian life, as we noted earlier. Archaeologist Kathryn Bard writes: "The Nile was ancient Egypt's most important natural resource. Within the Nile Valley and Delta, with the adjacent low deserts, all of the basic resources that sustained human life were available—water, food, and the raw materials for tools, clothing, and shelter."[1] Egypt was dependent on the annual inundation of the Nile for its prosperity, so any portent, as in a dream, that appeared to threaten that regular inundation was very serious, especially for Pharaoh, who was regarded as a godlike guardian of the Nile in cooperation with the god of the Nile inundation, Hapy. The Pharaoh Akhenaten called himself "a Nile for his people."

Any breakdown in the regularity of the Nile flooding would reflect on the competence of the pharaoh to maintain cosmic order, for the chief responsibility of the pharaoh was to maintain ma'at, universal harmony, in the country as an intermediary between the gods and his people. The goddess Ma'at (pronounced *may-et* or *my-eht*) was thought to work her will through the pharaoh, but it was up to the individual ruler to interpret the goddess's will correctly and then to act on it. One of the pharaoh's responsibilities was to maintain records of the level of the Nile. No wonder he was disturbed by his dreams. He would have understood them as a message from the gods that fairly obviously boded no good—but what message?

Hapy (or Hapi) was the god of the Nile (more precisely, of the Nile inundation) and the Egyptians associated him with the various primeval creation gods. Hapy is depicted holding a lotus and a papyrus to show his dominion over the entire Nile. He is portrayed as a fat man with female breasts to emphasize his fertility. The inundation of the Nile was called "the arrival of Hapy."

---

1. *Introduction to the Archaelogy of Ancient Egypt* (Oxford, UK: Blackwell, 2007), 67.

Pharaoh just had to know what the dreams meant, and he responded to Joseph's assurance that God (whoever he might be) could interpret his dreams by relating them to Joseph.

In the first dream, seven fat cows came up from the Nile to feed but were gruesomely devoured by seven lean and ugly cows that appeared after them. The strange thing was that the ugly cows remained lean even after the feast.[2] In the second dream, the king saw seven healthy ears of corn growing on a single stalk that were devoured by seven withered and unhealthy ears that appeared after them.

Pharaoh admitted to Joseph that none of his experts could make sense of the dreams. It may well be that they suspected the dreams meant ill for Pharaoh and the land that depended so much on the Nile, and, reluctant to be the bearers of bad news, they prudently chose to remain silent.

Joseph, however, did not hesitate and explained to the king that both dreams meant the same thing. As with the dreams of the cupbearer and the baker, the numbers in them are time indicators. They constituted a message from God that there would be seven years of plenty in the land followed by seven years of famine. Just as a large cat in the Egyptian book of dreams symbolized a large harvest, so did a large cow.

The fact that God had sent the same message twice signified, in Joseph's words, that the seven years of plenty followed by seven of famine was "fixed by God, and God will shortly bring it about" (41:32).

We know from other ancient sources that famines caused by failure of the annual inundation, even some lasting seven years, as here, were not unknown in Egypt. But one that was predicted seven years in advance was unprecedented.

Pharaoh now knew that Joseph was a man of a kind he had never met before, a man whose God had revealed the meaning of

---

2. The word for the reeds among which the cows grazed is an Egyptian word. This serves as a note of authenticity.

the dreams he had sent to the king. Pharaoh also knew that the God of Joseph had the power to intervene in human affairs. What that subsequently meant for Pharaoh's understanding of God we do not know.

Certainly Pharaoh was being confronted head-on with the existence of a hitherto unknown supernatural dimension, and he may well have wondered how a Hebrew slave and prison manager could have knowledge that he, the god-like pharaoh, and all of his top advisors did not have.

The message from God was devastating. In a sense it constituted an affront on the Egyptian concept of *ma'at*, order, which Pharaoh was responsible to maintain. In another sense, what was going to happen could be seen as an attack on the river god Hapy, or worse still, as evidence that he did not exist. Hapy would be seen as no longer able to supply the needs of the people as expressed in the so-called Hymn to the Nile: "So it is, Oh Nile, verdant art thou, who makest man and cattle to live."[3]

A few centuries later Moses would confront another pharaoh of a very different character, whose antagonism to God was such that God plagued Egypt with a series of plagues designed to attack a whole array of Egyptian gods. Exodus 12:12 says: "On all the gods of Egypt I will execute judgments." At that time Moses would be concerned to deliver Israel from Egypt. Here Joseph was concerned to deliver Egypt and Israel from starvation.

One can imagine that Pharaoh was horrified, feeling in the grip of forces that he could not understand, let alone control. How would he restore ma'at? Furthermore, he would have been overwhelmed with the fact that this foreign prisoner appeared to have more knowledge of and control over the Nile than he did as pharaoh. The God that Joseph had mentioned was clearly in a different category from Hapy.

3. See John D. Currid, *Ancient Egypt and the Old Testament* (Grand Rapids, MI: Baker, 1997), 110.

But Joseph had not finished. He would now answer Pharaoh's unspoken question: What do I need to do in light of this prediction? Joseph proceeded to give advice to Pharaoh about how to restore *ma'at*. He should plan for what was about to happen by appointing a wise leader over the land to organize a 20 percent grain tax during the years of plenty, which would be housed in store cities as a reserve for when the famine came.

Joseph had run Potiphar's house and the king's prison and clearly learned a lot about practical economics. He saw that what he had learned could be scaled up, and he did so. He had had a good apprenticeship for running an empire.

Pharaoh was no fool and rapidly saw, first, that he had an administrative genius in front of him and, second, that Joseph's plan would be effective, not only to secure the food supply for the nation but also to consolidate and enhance Pharaoh's own power over the nation by putting everyone deeply in his debt. Pharaoh may even have suspected that Joseph was giving him a strong hint as to what to do, even in his own interests.

No wonder, then, that "this proposal pleased Pharaoh and all his servants. And Pharaoh said to his servants, 'Can we find a man like this, in whom is the Spirit of God?'" (Gen. 41:37–38). Whatever Pharaoh meant by the word "God," it may be that he sensed a supernatural dimension to what had just happened. After all, the inundation of the Nile was (supposed to be) the province of the god Hapy in conjunction with Pharaoh himself. Or it may be that he was picking up on Joseph's reference to God to lend supernatural authority to the appointment he was about to make in order to get it past his senior ministers. He was about to elevate a foreigner, indeed a slave who had been accused of rape, straight out of prison, to become grand vizier, and he did not want anyone blocking it. There is a subtlety in this dialogue that is intriguingly difficult to fathom.

Perhaps the best insight into what is at stake here is given to us by a text in Ezekiel 29 that speaks about a later pharaoh:

In the tenth year, in the tenth month, on the twelfth day of the month, the word of the LORD came to me: "Son of man, set your face against Pharaoh king of Egypt, and prophesy against him and against all Egypt; speak, and say, Thus says the Lord GOD:

"Behold, I am against you,
     Pharaoh king of Egypt,
the great dragon that lies
     in the midst of his streams,
that says, 'My Nile is my own;
     I made it for myself.'" . . .

"Because you said, 'The Nile is mine, and I made it,' therefore, behold, I am against you and against your streams, and I will make the land of Egypt an utter waste and desolation, from Migdol to Syene, as far as the border of Cush. No foot of man shall pass through it, and no foot of beast shall pass through it; it shall be uninhabited forty years." (vv. 1–3, 9–11)

God remonstrates with Pharaoh because of Pharaoh's blasphemous pretention not only to have been the creator of the Nile but to have created it for himself. Therefore the major issue is clearly the breaking of the first commandment: "You shall have no other gods before me" (Ex. 20:3). God through Joseph was teaching Pharaoh a basic lesson in this direction. Through Moses God would teach a later pharaoh much more as that pharaoh wrestled with whether to release Israel from Egyptian oppression.

This pharaoh had made his decision. In spite of the fact that there was as yet no evidence that Joseph was right (how could there have been in the nature of things?), no evidence of a coming extended famine, or indeed, of seven continuous years of plenty, he decided there and then that there was enough evidence to trust Joseph.

There was also the fact that Joseph had said, "God will give Pharaoh a favorable answer" (Gen. 41:16). The king had been deeply troubled by his dreams. Now he had peace about the situation, a peace that came from God, and it assured Pharaoh of the genuineness of what he was learning.

Not only that, but Joseph had spoken with great authority. Like Daniel centuries later, he clearly believed what he was saying both about the source and the meaning of the dreams. After all, it was obvious that, for Joseph, everything depended on it. And Pharaoh had the sense to realize that in Joseph there was the Spirit of God.

We have here reached a high point of witness: Joseph confidently doing what the God of Abraham, Isaac, and Jacob had intended for the nation—making God's name known to the world.

We are called upon to do the same, and the clear lesson arising from what we are now reading is that the authenticity and authority of our witness depends on our conviction that the message we have to proclaim is of God and is true. We are not (normally) called upon to interpret dreams, but we are instructed, indeed, commanded to preach the Word of God. And there is no way that we shall have any traction unless we are convinced of the truth of the message that we preach.

Yet particularly in the West, we are losing our confidence in the gospel—an attitude symptomatic of the spirit of the age. In their book *Suicide of the West*, Richard Koch and Chris Smith suggest that there has been a collapse of Western self-confidence that has little to do with enemies and everything to do with seismic shifts in ideas and attitudes.

They ascribe the success of the West hitherto to six principal ideas: Christianity, optimism, science, economic growth, liberalism, and individualism. These, they aver, have suffered a century of sustained attack, and now where cynicism, pessimism, and carelessness abound, a drift toward collective suicide is evident. Their take on Christianity is fascinating:

> Christianity comprised one overarching belief. . . . The overarching belief was that God became man, lived, suffered, died and rejoined the divine realm. This wonderful news moved

humankind and God together. . . . As a result the whole course
of human history and the potential fate of everyone on earth,
shifted immeasurably for the better. "The *Logos* became flesh
and dwelt among us," revealing God's infinite love for human
kind. Because of this single event, the eternal became historical,
the divine became personal, and individual lives—even those
of quite unexceptional ordinary folk—became supremely important. All men and women could access the divine nature,
the Spirit of God could dwell within them.[4]

These ideas promoted personal responsibilities, using Christ's
power to change, helping the underdog and saving the lost. What
has happened? The authors say, "Because the West took science
and rational investigation further than any other civilization—inspired largely by a Christian desire to celebrate and understand
God's creation—it was also the first to move towards a secular
society."[5]

Here is the story as often told today: science moved the focus
from God to nature and humanity. Copernicus (1473–1543)
moved the earth from the center of creation. Through advances
in celestial mechanics (Newton, seventeenth century) God was
reduced to a celestial deistic watchmaker. Darwin (1809–1882)
removed the speciality of humans as made in the image of God and
demoted them to animals made by unguided natural processes.
Nietzsche (1844–1900) announced the death of God. Science had
demoted and finally banished God.[6]

As the poet Robert Browning (1812–1889) said, "We have
moved from an age of faith diversified by doubt to an age of doubt
diversified by faith."

All this means that confidence in God and in the Lord and the
gospel is being shaken as never before. We need to put against that

---

4. Richard Koch and Chris Smith, *Suicide of the West* (London: Continuum, 2006), n.p.
5. Ibid.
6. In my *God's Undertaker: Has Science Buried God?* (Oxford, UK: Lion Hudson, 2009),
I argue that this is not so. In fact science strengthens the case for God.

the fact that Joseph was a single individual, with no other human group supporting him, yet such was his conviction of the truth of the message he had to communicate that he influenced the future of an entire nation. That is the sort of confidence in God and his Word that is necessary in order to stand up and reverse the trend of weakness and lack of conviction and authenticity that characterize far too much of that which calls itself Christian. Joseph was confident, authentic, and convincing.

> Then Pharaoh said to Joseph, "Since God has shown you all this, there is none so discerning and wise as you are. You shall be over my house, and all my people shall order themselves as you command. Only as regards the throne will I be greater than you." And Pharaoh said to Joseph, "See, I have set you over all the land of Egypt." Then Pharaoh took his signet ring from his hand and put it on Joseph's hand, and clothed him in garments of fine linen and put a gold chain about his neck. And he made him ride in his second chariot. And they called out before him, "Bow the knee!" Thus he set him over all the land of Egypt. (41:39–43)

The matter of the trust that one person puts in another has come up several times in the narrative. Jacob trusted Joseph to report on his brothers, Potiphar trusted Joseph with his household affairs, the jailor trusted Joseph with the prisoners, and now Pharaoh has decided to trust the cupbearer's account of Joseph's interpretation of his dream and in consequence to trust Joseph not only with the interpretation of his own dreams but with the hugely responsible task of running the economy of Egypt.

The dreams of both cupbearer and Pharaoh had to do with time—the first, a short period of three days; and the second, a protracted period of fourteen years, seven of plenty, seven of famine. Did Pharaoh reason to himself that since Joseph had been proved right about the meaning of the cupbearer's dream, he was likely to be right about the dreams of Pharaoh?

The confirmation of prediction plays an important role in the wider context of the validation of Christianity where we also have the evidence of the fulfillment of both short-term and long-term predictions, or prophecies. This is one reason that the Christmas story, as communicated in countless carol services around the world, is so powerful and memorable. The readings from Scripture that interweave with the inspiring carols are replete with fulfilled prophecy: a virgin conceiving, a child born in Bethlehem whose goings forth are from everlasting (Mic. 5:2), and even the Wise Men guided to the manger in Bethlehem by a star.

Jesus himself made short-term predictions:

> So the Jews said to him, "What sign do you show us for doing these things?" Jesus answered them, "Destroy this temple, and in three days I will raise it up." The Jews then said, "It has taken forty-six years to build this temple, and will you raise it up in three days?" But he was speaking about the temple of his body. When therefore he was raised from the dead, his disciples remembered that he had said this, and they believed the Scripture and the word that Jesus had spoken. (John 2:18–22)

Roughly three years after this prediction Jesus rose from the dead on the third day, and his disciples' faith in him was strengthened by their recollection that he had told them beforehand.

Pharaoh had acted very swiftly to perform one of the most remarkable promotions in history—taking Joseph from imprisoned slave administrator to governor of the entire country. The only other instance of anything remotely like it is the case of Daniel.

Now, at long last, as Joseph is catapulted into the public arena, we begin to see the first evidences of the promised blessing that the seed of Abraham could and would bring to the world. Pharaoh is so convinced of Joseph's authenticity and capability that he invests him with virtually unlimited authority over the nation. Joseph is to be obeyed without question by every citizen. His only superior is the king himself on his throne. The masses of Egyptians bowed to him, yet they had not been the subjects of his teenage dreams. One cannot help wondering, in passing, how Potiphar and his wife reacted to Joseph being elevated far above them in power and social standing, for they had to bow also. This was a dramatic example of God's principle: "Those who honor me I will honor" (1 Sam. 2:30). God had vindicated Joseph at the highest possible level.

Yes, Joseph was vindicated. Does that mean that all believers who have suffered false accusation, vilification, discrimination, and even imprisonment will live to see vindication? Is lack of vindication an evidence of guilt? History shows us all too clearly that this is not the case. Some are called to "be faithful unto death" (Rev. 2:10), whose vindication will come only after death. Our Lord is the supreme example, and the first martyr, Stephen, is another.

The elevation of a person of Semitic origin to a position of great authority in ancient Egypt is not without historical precedent. Westermann writes that the installation of Joseph "is an event that we can visualise in all its details as very few others in the Bible. Every detail of the ceremony has been passed down to us in Egyptian representations, even down to the almost transparent linen garments. We can view the rings, the golden chains and the war chariots in the museums."[7]

Joseph had passed with flying colors the tests of coping with social ostracism and suffering. Now he has to learn to cope with the exact opposite—wealth, status, and fame. He went straight from the bottom to the top at a speed calculated to make anyone else giddy and disoriented.

How do we cope with wealth, status, and fame, if we have it? For God does give it to some believers, as he did to Joseph. Though we are told in Scripture that there are "not many . . . powerful, not many . . . of noble birth" (1 Cor. 1:26), we are not told that there aren't any. It would be a mistake to think of wealth merely

7. C. Westermann, *Genesis 37–50*, Biblisches Kommentar: Altes Testament (Neukirchener Verlag, 1974–1982), 3:97.

in monetary terms, for although God has gifted many believers with business acumen, there is a wealth of intellect and inventive and practical skills in many fields—gifts of artistic, musical, and literary ability—and a wealth of personality, relational, and organizational talent.

We are called upon to accept such gifts as from God and to use them in his service and for the benefit of others, but not to trust them, as we saw earlier in connection with Joseph's work ethic. Money is a root of all kinds of evil, but in the hands of believers who regard themselves as stewards under God, money can be a source of all kinds of good. The early church was certainly grateful to have believers who could afford a home large enough to house a church.

Joseph's promotion brought immense prosperity and power. It also brought his renaming by Pharaoh as Zaphenath-paneah, the meaning of which is uncertain but could be something like "God speaks, he lives," or "revealer of hidden things." If so, it was certainly appropriate.

Joseph's promotion brought a marriage, again arranged by Pharaoh, into a prominent Egyptian priestly family, to Asenath ("she who belongs to the goddess Neit"), the daughter of Potiphera, priest of On. It is somewhat ironic that Joseph's father-in-law should have almost the same name as the man who bought him as a slave. Potiphera means "he whom Re [or Ra, the sun god] has given." The center of the worship of Ra was On (Heliopolis, the city of the sun) lying ten miles northeast of Cairo.[8]

It was an extraordinary situation. Joseph was now son-in-law to a man who was, presumably, a high-ranking and influential pagan priest. The marriage raises obvious questions. Was it right for Joseph as a believer to marry an unbeliever from a foreign nation? However, we are given no more information as to the status

---

8. For detailed discussion of these names see K. A. Kitchen, *On the Reliability of the Old Testament* (Grand Rapids, MI: Eerdmans, 2003), 344.

of her belief; she may even have been a convert to Joseph's God, as one Jewish tradition has it.

In any case, even if she was not (yet) a believer, Joseph does not appear to have had any choice in the matter, and there is no criticism of him in the text for having married her. Maybe the lesson we need to learn is that though it is God's stated ideal—indeed, command—that a believer should not marry an unbeliever, he, in his merciful providence, can help people to overcome even in a situation that is far from ideal that may be none of their own making.

With his home base firmly established, Joseph threw himself into the task of administering the nation's agriculture with immense success. "Joseph stored up grain in great abundance, like the sand of the sea, until he ceased to measure it, for it could not be measured" (Gen. 41:49). The narrative throws up certain questions. The original economic austerity plan suggested by Joseph involved a grain tax of 20 percent. However, we now read that Joseph gathered up *all* the food and put it in store in the cities. This seems to be a draconian measure and leaves us wondering about the plight of the average farmer. How could those in the countryside live if all the grain was taken far away from them? Or does "all the food" (v. 48) simply mean all that was demanded under the tax? Whatever the answer, the result was immensely profitable and led to grain unmeasurable, like the sand of the sea. That metaphor has appeared before in Genesis but used of the seed of Abraham as that which would bless the whole world (32:12). We are, therefore, led to think of two different kinds of seed.

Six years passed, and the next landmark in Joseph's life concerned his own seed: he started a family. Two children were born:

Before the year of famine came, two sons were born to Joseph. Asenath, the daughter of Potiphera priest of On, bore them to him. Joseph called the name of the firstborn Manasseh. "For," he said, "God has made me forget all my hardship and all my

father's house." The name of the second he called Ephraim,
"For God has made me fruitful in the land of my affliction."
(41:50–52)

The fact that the two sons were given Hebrew names and subsequently took their place as tribal leaders in Israel on a par with
Joseph's brothers may well be evidence that Asenath had indeed
become a believer. We note that the two names record the two
phases of Joseph's life of suffering—the hardship of his father's
house and the affliction of Egypt. They were never to be forgotten, so long as Israel existed as a nation. Indeed, calling his child
Manasseh ("he who causes to forget") of course means he would
never forget. There is no way in which he can shut out the past,
and Manasseh's very name will be a constant reminder of it. In
fact, it will not be long before he has a head-on confrontation with
that past when his brothers arrive in Egypt.

The name of his firstborn child—"God has made me forget *all*
. . . my father's house"—raises another question. We can perhaps
understand his desire to forget his ten brothers who hated him, but
what about his father and, indeed, his younger brother Benjamin?
Was there a desire to forget his father? And if so, why? Certainly,
since Joseph had come to power, he had made no effort to contact
his father and inform him that he was still alive. He could easily
have dispatched a messenger to do so. Had Joseph during his years
as a slave begun to blame Jacob and resent the favoritism he'd
been shown as a boy that so incensed his brothers? In addition,
had he culturally left "his father's house" in the sense that he had,
to all intents and purposes, become an Egyptian, apart from his
faith in God?

Once more we run up against a tantalizing lack of information
and the (understandable) tendency of some commentators to write
as if Joseph were a flawlessly pious human being, since they can
find no criticism of him in the biblical narrative. In the end we
simply do not know, but it is not difficult to imagine that at least

there was some cultural tension in his thinking. His background must by now have seemed remote; he was happily married to an Egyptian; he had a family, great prestige and wealth, and a secure position and future in the Egyptian empire.

Despite all that, he was soon to be confronted with his past in an unexpected and dramatic way that would eventually change his life forever. It was the predicted famine that triggered that confrontation.

The famine set in as Joseph had foretold to Pharaoh seven years before. The fact that it did, right on cue, would have done much to establish Joseph's authority. He had gotten the interpretation right. One wonders about the discussion this gave rise to in intellectual circles in Egypt. It was a serious famine, not only confined to Egypt but affecting the surrounding nations. Egypt had bread, but the nations did not, and so, as the famine intensified, they were forced to travel to Egypt to try to buy food supplies. The money flowed in to Pharaoh's coffers and increased his wealth, and no doubt that of Joseph as well, yet more.

Some think that Joseph's support of an increase in the despotic power of the king is highly problematic. Or is it possible that Joseph managed to keep his head because of the character he had developed through unjust suffering for so long? Again, our information is inadequate.

15

The Path of Forgiveness and Reconciliation, Act 1

The famine in Egypt reached as far as Canaan on the Mediterranean coast, around two hundred miles away. Jacob somehow heard that there was grain for sale in Egypt and called his sons together to ask them to go down to Egypt and buy. He did not allow Benjamin, Joseph's brother, to go, even though Benjamin was an adult. Perhaps Jacob had been having suspicions about the brothers' account of Joseph's death and was wary of their attitude toward Benjamin.

He therefore sent the ten remaining brothers on their way. Without any inkling of what he was doing, he set in motion a train of events that would take his family into Egypt and shape the future of his nation. Abraham had gone to Egypt for a short time because of famine, and Isaac had nearly done the same. What was about to happen to Jacob and his family was in a completely different category in terms of its historical significance.

> Now Joseph was governor over the land. He was the one who sold to all the people of the land. And Joseph's brothers came and bowed themselves before him with their faces to the ground. Joseph saw his brothers and recognized them,

but he treated them like strangers and spoke roughly to them. "Where do you come from?" he said. They said, "From the land of Canaan, to buy food." And Joseph recognized his brothers, but they did not recognize him. And Joseph remembered the dreams that he had dreamed of them. (Gen. 42:6–9)

It is not surprising that the brothers did not recognize Joseph as he stood before them looking every inch the clean-shaven Egyptian aristocrat surrounded by guards and functionaries.

It is hard to imagine the swirling mixture of emotions that affected Joseph as it dawned on him that the ten bearded men bunched in the crowd in front of him were his brothers whom he had not seen for well over twenty years. He watched them bow, and, in that moment, a boyhood dream became a reality. Yet not quite. Every detail of that dream would have been indelibly etched on his memory. In it he had seen eleven sheaves bow down, but he saw only ten men bowing in front of him. Where was his brother Benjamin? How was he to deal with these men who had caused him so much pain and suffering? Once they had been in a position of power over him. Now the situation was reversed. Was there a right action for him to take?

The roughness in his voice as he asked them where they had come from must have disconcerted them. After all, they wanted only to engage in the simple transaction of buying some food and starting back home.

They were even more disturbed when the Egyptian prince accused them of spying: "Joseph remembered the dreams that he had dreamed of them. And he said to them, 'You are spies; you have come to see the nakedness of the land'" (42:9). They were vulnerable visitors to a foreign country with a different language and customs. In that context, to be accused of spying was an extremely frightening experience—who knew what the outcome would be? The men were quick to protest and replied, "No, my lord, your servants have come to buy food. We are all sons of one

man. We are honest men. Your servants have never been spies"
(42:10–11).

They repeat the purpose of their mission. They add that they
are all from a single family, presumably to settle any suspicion that
they are a gang up to no good. They protest that they are honest
men who have never been spies. Presumably they had never been
spies, but honest men? That was a different matter. We know that
for years they had maintained to their father the lie that Joseph
was dead.

Why the roughness in Joseph's voice and attitude? Was this
evidence of a man who couldn't wait to get revenge and punish
those who had caused him years of pain and deprivation? If it
were, which of us could blame him? The desire to hit back is not
far beneath the surface in the fallen human psyche, and handling
it is not at all easy at the best of times. Or was it more than that,
the beginning of a well-thought-out plan of action designed by
Joseph to get his brothers to face what they had done and its consequences? Or might it have been a mixture of both? Again, we
do not have enough information to give a definitive answer. What
we can say for sure is that the biblical instructions to believers in
this situation are clear:

> Repay no one evil for evil, but give thought to do what is
> honorable in the sight of all. If possible, so far as it depends on
> you, live peaceably with all. Beloved, never avenge yourselves,
> but leave it to the wrath of God, for it is written, "Vengeance
> is mine, I will repay, says the Lord." To the contrary, "if your
> enemy is hungry, feed him; if he is thirsty, give him something
> to drink; for by so doing you will heap burning coals on his
> head." Do not be overcome by evil, but overcome evil with
> good. (Rom. 12:17–21)

Here were men looking to buy food. They could certainly be
fitted into the category of Joseph's enemies, so an argument could
be made that he should have simply left vengeance to God, given

them the grain, taken their money, and let them go. However, what would that have achieved? Would it have overcome evil with good?

What complicates a straightforward application of Romans 12 to Joseph's situation is, first, the fact that Romans 12 is written to Christians; it is not written in the context of Old Testament times where, from time to time, God delegated the exercise of his judgment to his people Israel—and indeed to other tribes and nations. Second, anger is often an expression of sin but is not necessarily so: "Be angry and do not sin," says Paul (Eph. 4:26). We do not know whether Joseph was angry with his brothers at this point, but what becomes increasingly clear is that it is more likely, as we suggested above, that Joseph's actions are part of a plan to bring his brothers to face their guilty past and repent of it with a view to forgiveness and reconciliation.

They claimed to be honest men. Joseph would put that to the test. He piled on the pressure: "He said to them, 'No, it is the nakedness of the land that you have come to see'" (Gen. 42:12). This renewed accusation of spying forced them to say more: "We, your servants, are twelve brothers, the sons of one man in the land of Canaan, and behold, the youngest is this day with our father, and one is no more" (42:13).

Joseph now knew, that is, if they were telling the truth, that both his father and his younger brother Benjamin were still alive. The hope of seeing them again must have been overpowering. He also knew that they believed that he, Joseph, was "no more," that is, dead. That admission certainly made it less likely that they had also done away with Benjamin and that Jacob was dead. It also meant that they had no idea who he, Joseph, was. They certainly had not come to Egypt in the hope of finding him.

Joseph ramped up the pressure yet more: "'It is as I said to you. You are spies. By this you shall be tested: by the life of Pharaoh, you shall not go from this place unless your youngest brother comes here. Send one of you, and let him bring your brother, while you remain confined, that your words may be tested, whether there is truth in you. Or else, by the life of Pharaoh, surely you are spies.' And he put them all together in custody for three days" (42:14–17). Swearing twice by the life of Pharaoh was intended to scare them by its intensity.

How this additional information about their family showed, or indeed could have shown, that they were spies is questionable. And how bringing their younger brother would establish that they were not spies is equally problematic.

There is an interesting matter of translation here. Rather than the vague "It is as I said to you," Yuval Levin suggests that the closer translation should be something like, "He is it that I spoke unto you"; that is, Joseph is picking up on their reference to his being "no more." Thus, the meaning would be "He's the one I am talking about. It's because of him I say you are spies."[1]

If so, how were they to understand the reference? Certainly, if they were to bring their younger brother, it would show that they were at least speaking the truth on that issue. And Joseph had expressed interest in testing whether there was truth in them. The apparent superficiality of the logic regarding spying points toward a deeper motivation—that of determining what the brothers really felt about Benjamin, Joseph's full brother.

The men who had callously imprisoned Joseph in the empty water cistern in the desert found themselves in prison. Their thoughts troubled them deeply. Their father thought Joseph was dead. He had kept Benjamin at home and let the other ten sons go to Egypt. What would Jacob do if only one were to return and demand to take Benjamin away so that he ran the risk of losing all twelve? Jacob would never let Benjamin go under such perilous circumstances. And if he didn't, the future of the nine men left in Egypt in prison was an unthinkable nightmare. Throughout history espionage has been regarded as a traitorous offense often punished with torture and death. These men were in deadly trouble.

---

1. Cited in Leon Kass, *The Beginning of Wisdom: Reading Genesis* (New York: Free Press, 2003), n.p.

Joseph had been through the fire of testing himself: "The word of the LORD tested him" (Ps. 105:19). He was applying pressure to these men, to test them to see if their words were true. He let them stew for three days, a very short time compared with the years Joseph himself had spent in a prison because of their hatred of him. He then had them brought out, and he made a conciliatory gesture:

> Joseph said to them, "Do this and you will live, for I fear God: if you are honest men, let one of your brothers remain confined where you are in custody, and let the rest go and carry grain for the famine of your households, and bring your youngest brother to me. So your words will be verified, and you shall not die." (Gen. 42:18–20)

What could this Egyptian mean by saying he "feared God"? Which God? Could he have some knowledge of the God of Jacob? It was scarcely thinkable. Yet he was being more generous than the brothers had been led to expect. Then he ordered only one brother to be kept hostage, while the remaining nine could return with food and fetch the youngest.

Their consciences had been active over the preceding days, and they started to talk among themselves in their own language, unaware that Joseph could understand every word.

> Then they said to one another, "In truth we are guilty concerning our brother, in that we saw the distress of his soul, when he begged us and we did not listen. That is why this distress has come upon us." And Reuben answered them, "Did I not tell you not to sin against the boy? But you did not listen. So now there comes a reckoning for his blood." They did not know that Joseph understood them, for there was an interpreter between them. (42:21–23)

Under the pressure of the situation, their long-buried guilt broke the surface, and they admitted it openly among themselves as they recalled Joseph's distress when he had begged them to free him from the cistern years before. As Joseph listened, he detected the first signs of honesty in his brothers: "In truth we are guilty." He also learned that Reuben, Jacob's firstborn, had tried in vain to save him, indicating that the brothers were not equally guilty.

Circumstances can force guilt to the surface in any of us. We know that Joseph's actions do that in his brothers, but one cannot help thinking that there are times when God does the same thing to us. In his providential care, he so arranges our circumstances that we are forced to face things we have suppressed or tried to forget that we need to deal with in order to grow as believers both morally and spiritually. Looking back over life, can you think of instances when you were brought to face and deal with guilt through circumstances for which you now thank God?

Hearing his brothers' confession of guilt was too much for Joseph. Overcome with emotion, he turned away from them and wept (42:24). This is the first time we read of Joseph weeping. It will not be the last. It reveals to us something of his heart. This is scarcely the reaction of a cruel, vindictive man, toying with his brothers, reveling in their pain as he seeks to get the maximum revenge for what they had done to him. This is much more the attitude of a man who wanted to forgive and be reconciled. He wanted to tell them who he was, but he couldn't do it yet. Why not? Because Joseph knew that genuine forgiveness involves repentance.

16

The Nature of Forgiveness

At this point in the story of Joseph, we come to the heart of a very sensitive topic on which there is considerable disagreement and even confusion both among believers and the public at large. It was C. S. Lewis who observed: "Every one says forgiveness is a lovely idea, until they have something to forgive."[1] So please be patient with me as I try to explain, as clearly as I can, what I think that Scripture has to say on this topic. At the very least it should give readers something to discuss.

First, consider the following tragic incident. A newspaper report at the time of the London Tube bombings on July 7, 2005, relays the tragic loss of a twenty-four-year-old woman and her mother's inability to forgive those responsible. The mother of the young woman said, "I do not forgive them for what they did and I do not think they should be forgiven."[2] Ten years later she said she still could not forgive the suicide bombers.

Should she have taken this path? Or should she have responded like Gordon Wilson, whose daughter Marie was killed in the

---

1. C. S. Lewis, *The Best of C. S. Lewis: Five Complete Books in One Volume* (Washington, DC: Canon Press, 1969), 492.

2. "Priest 'Cannot Forgive' Bombers," *BBC News* website, July 7, 2006, accessed November 8, 2018, http://news.bbc.co.uk/2/hi/uk_news/england/bristol/somerset/5156972.stm.

Enniskillen bombing in 1987? He said he prayed for the bombers every day: "I bear no ill-will, I bear no grudge." His tribute to his daughter has gone down as one of the most moving in all the years of the conflict in Northern Ireland. His book is called *Marie: Story from Enniskillen*.[3]

Or we might think about the response of the Amish community to the West Nickel Mines School shooting on October 2, 2006, in which five girls were killed by Charles Roberts. Jack Meyer, a member of the local Brethren community, said: "I don't think there's anybody here that wants to do anything but forgive and not only reach out to those who have suffered a loss in that way but to reach out to the family of the man who committed these acts."[4] Marie Roberts, the widow of the killer, wrote an open letter to her Amish neighbors thanking them for their forgiveness, grace, and mercy. Donald Kraybill and two other scholars of Amish life noted that "letting go of grudges" is a deeply rooted value in Amish culture.[5] They explained that the Amish willingness to forgo vengeance does not undo the tragedy or pardon the wrong but rather constitutes a first step toward a future that is more hopeful.

Then again, there is the famous book *The Sunflower: On the Possibilities and Limits of Forgiveness* by Nazi hunter Simon Wiesenthal.[6] In it he tells how as a Jewish prisoner in a concentration camp he was summoned to the deathbed of a Nazi soldier who asked him for forgiveness. Wiesenthal left the room without a word. Years after the war had ended Wiesenthal asked himself whether he had done the right thing. In the book fifty-three distinguished men and women respond to his questions with very varied responses.

---

3. Gordon Wilson and Alf McCreary, *Marie: Story from Enniskillen* (London: Marshall Pickering, 1990).

4. Cited in Adrian Raine, *The Anatomy of Violence: The Biological Roots of Crime* (New York: Vintage, 2013), 323–24.

5. See "Amish Grandfather: 'We Must Not Think Evil of This Man,'" KLTV website, October 4, 2006, accessed November 8, 2018, http://www.kltv.com/story/5495980/amish -grandfather-we-must-not-think-evil-of-this-man/.

6. Simon Wiesenthal, *The Sunflower: On the Possibilities and Limits of Forgiveness*, exp. ed. (New York: Schocken, 1998).

How are we to understand all of this?

Forgiveness lies at the heart of the gospel itself. The basic terms of the gospel are very clear. In Luke 24:47 our Lord tells the disciples that "repentance for the forgiveness of sins should be proclaimed in his name to all nations, beginning from Jerusalem." In the first public proclamation of the gospel in Jerusalem on the day of Pentecost Peter commanded his hearers, "Repent and be baptized every one of you in the name of Jesus Christ for the forgiveness of your sins" (Acts 2:38). A few days later he preached: "Repent therefore, and turn back, that your sins may be blotted out" (Acts 3:19). Some years later Paul explained to King Agrippa, "I . . . declared . . . that they should repent and turn to God, performing deeds in keeping with their repentance" (Acts 26:19–20).

It is therefore clear that the basis of forgiveness is repentance toward God and faith in the Lord Jesus. At the fundamental level there appears to be no forgiveness without repentance. Jesus himself said, "Unless you repent, you will all likewise perish" (Luke 13:3).

These ideas are reflected in our Lord's and Paul's instructions about forgiveness between fellow Christians. Paul writes in Ephesians 4:32: "Be kind to one another, tenderhearted, forgiving one another, as God in Christ forgave you." He uses the term *charizomai*, which emphasizes the grace of God in forgiveness. The Lord, in Luke 17:3–4, says, "If your brother sins, rebuke him, and if he repents, forgive him, and if he sins against you seven times in the day, and turns to you seven times, saying, 'I repent,' you must forgive him."

The parallel passage in Matthew 18 does not use the word *repentance* but tells a parable about a king settling accounts with debtors. One man owes ten thousand denarii, and the king threatens him and his family with slavery to pay the debt. The debtor begs for time to pay, and out of pity the master forgives him the entire debt. But then the forgiven servant finds someone who owes him just one hundred denarii and demands repayment. When the man pleads with him, the forgiven servant is indifferent and has the man imprisoned. The servants report the incident to the master, who is furious at the servant's unforgiving attitude and puts him back in prison until he pays the entire debt. The application is: "So also my heavenly Father will do to every one of you, if you do not forgive your brother from your heart" (v. 35).

The main word translated "forgive" in the Gospels has a range of meanings: let go, leave, tolerate, permit, send away, release, cancel, pardon, and forgive. This is reflected in the *Oxford English Dictionary's* definition of forgiveness: (1) "To give up, to cease to harbour, resentment; disposition or willingness to forgive; (2) to remit (or let go a debt), to pardon an offender."[7]

Forgiveness appears to have at least two aspects: (1) the inner life of the injured party, an inward letting go; (2) the outward relation of the injured party to the one who has committed the offense, an outward letting go where the offender is explicitly pardoned.

We get both aspects in Scripture. First, in Mark 11:25 Jesus says: "Whenever you stand praying, forgive, if you have anything against anyone, so that your Father also who is in heaven may forgive you your trespasses." The person who has injured you is not necessarily present, so it cannot be a question of publicly letting the matter go. Christ is here addressing the danger that our prayers and our lives will be damaged by harboring resentment and an unforgiving spirit. The first level of forgiveness, then, is that inner letting go.

And that may be difficult, especially for people who have experienced deep cruelty, abuse, and hurt. Yet the one who encourages us to do it is the Lord himself, who gave us an example to follow: "When he suffered, he did not threaten" (1 Pet. 2:23). That does not mean, however, that he did not believe in judgment. On the contrary, as Peter tells us, the Lord committed himself to him who judges justly (v. 23). In that spirit, we are asked to follow the Lord and not to avenge ourselves: "'Vengeance is mine, I will repay,'

---

7. *Oxford English Dictionary*, 3rd ed., s.v. forgiveness.

says the Lord" (Rom. 12:19; see also Heb. 10:30). The preparation for offering forgiveness, in the sense of offering pardon and cancellation of debt, is letting the matter go inwardly so that it does not destroy the offended person.

However, saying to the offender, "I forgive you," is a different matter. If I've been wounded, if I'm the one who has to do the forgiving, I may well have to work hard at getting my heart right before the Lord and letting something go inwardly so that it does not fester and poison me. But that is not the same thing as an active pardon or remission of the guilt of the offender, nor is it the same as my relationship with them being reestablished, because that, according to Scripture, requires repentance on their part.

It is easy to forget that God himself does not forgive those who do not repent. "Unless you repent, you will all likewise perish," said our Lord in Luke 13:3, as we saw. The reason is surely a moral one. If God forgave people without repentance, he'd be saying that sin doesn't matter. But God will never say that sin doesn't matter. In light of this, to expect a mother to say to a terrorist who gives no evidence of repentance, "I forgive you for killing my daughter," could well be understood as suggesting that the offense does not really matter.

A distorted and cheap gospel that speaks about God's forgiveness without the need to turn away from sin and repent is no gospel at all. By effectively teaching that sin doesn't really matter because God forgives can actually be used to justify sinful, even criminal, behavior. A study carried out at Georgia State University bears this out. It gives evidence that criminals sometimes use religion to justify their crimes. Criminologists Volkan Topalli, Timothy Brezina, and Mindy Bernhardt published a paper entitled, "With God on My Side: The Paradoxical Relationship between Religious Belief and Criminality among Hardcore Street Offenders."[8] Here are a few sad examples of misunderstanding forgiveness that cropped

---

8. Volkan Topalli, Timothy Brezina, and Mindy Bernhardt, "With God on My Side: The Paradoxical Relationship between Religious Belief and Criminality among Hardcore Street Offenders," *Theoretical Criminology* 17.1 (2012): 49–69.

up in the interviews of forty-eight serious street offenders in the
Atlanta area on which the study was based.

> **Subject "Triggerman":** "No, no, no, I don't think that is right.
> I mean, anything can be forgiven. We live in Hell now and you
> can do anything [transgression] in Hell. When it all ends . . .
> we go up there [to Heaven] and the Devil comes down here.
> Only the Devil lives in Hell forever, man, all by his self. God
> has to forgive everyone, even if they don't believe in him."

> **Subject "Young Stunna":** "Well, you do get punished for doing
> wrong, but not if you don't have no choice. It's like this here.
> See, if I go and rob a m_____ then I'm still going to
> Heaven because . . . uhm . . . it's like, Jesus knows I ain't have
> no choice, you know? He know I got a decent heart."

> **Subject "Cool":** "The way it work is this. You go out and do
> some bad and then you ask for forgiveness and Jesus have to
> give it to you, and, you know, wipe the slate clean. So, I al-
> ways do a quick little prayer right before and then I'm cool
> with Jesus."[9]

Not surprisingly many atheist websites drew attention to this research to ridicule Christianity, failing to see that they are criticiz-
ing not genuine Christianity but a perversion of it.

Martin Luther wrote: "There are two kinds of sin: one is confessed, and this no one should leave unforgiven; the other kind is
defended, and this no one can forgive, for it refuses either to be
counted as sin or to accept forgiveness."[10]

"But," it is objected, "didn't the Lord Jesus, when he was
being crucified, pray, 'Father, forgive them, because they don't
know what they do'?" He did indeed. Notice, however, that his
words were addressed to people who did *not* know what they

9. See also http://coldcasechristianity.com/2013/does-belief-in-god-encourage-criminal
-behavior/.

10. Martin Luther, *Sermon on the Mount and Magnificat*, vol. 21, *Works of Martin
Luther*, ed. Helmut T. Lehmann (St. Louis, MO: Concordia, 1986), 153.

were doing. To apply them to people who knew exactly what they were doing makes no moral sense. The Roman soldiers for whom Christ prayed had no idea of the identity of the man they were crucifying. They understood themselves simply to be executing a condemned terrorist. So, in their hearing, the Lord prayed, "Father, forgive them," because once they woke up to the fact (and I expect some of them later did) that they had crucified the Son of God, it would have totally overwhelmed them, and they would have been overcome with remorse and repentance. That prayer showed them that there was grace for them also.

To apply the Lord's prayer for those soldiers to Julie Nicholson who lost her daughter in the London Tube bombings and insist that she forgive the terrorists publicly without their repentance would not be moral. Letting the hurt go inwardly is a completely different matter, and she records her struggles in her book.

The Lord also did not pray, "Father, forgive them," for those who, with eyes wide open, observed his deeds of miraculous mercy done through the power of the Holy Spirit and then attributed them to the Devil. On the contrary, he roundly told those Pharisees that for them, there could be no forgiveness "either in this age or in the age to come" (Matt. 12:32). There is sin so serious that, in the nature of things, it cannot be forgiven, by which I mean that if someone rejects the power of the Holy Spirit, who is the ultimate witness to the message of the gospel of the grace of God, then, by definition, there is no other power and no other gospel that can bring salvation.

It is tragic that, although Christ's death is sufficient for all and forgiveness is offered to all, some will find themselves eternally separated from God because they have not repented.

None of this means that forgiving even a repentant person is easy. Wiesenthal tells us that the dying Nazi who asked him for forgiveness had clearly repented. He still found it impossible to forgive. Many of his respondents supported that decision. The difficulty involved is graphically illustrated by Corrie ten Boom's account of being faced with a former prison guard. Here it is in her own words:

> And that's when I saw him, working his way forward against the others. One moment I saw the overcoat and the brown hat; the next, a blue uniform and a visored cap with its skull and crossbones. It came back with a rush. . . .
>
> The place was Ravensbruck [a concentration camp], and the man who was making his way forward had been a guard—one of the most cruel guards.
>
> Now he was in front of me, hand thrust out: "A fine message, Fräulein! How good it is to know that, as you say, all our sins are at the bottom of the sea!"
>
> And I, who had spoken so glibly of forgiveness, fumbled in my pocketbook rather than take that hand. He would not remember me, of course—how could he remember one prisoner among those thousands of women?
>
> But I remembered him. . . . I was face to face with one of my captors, and my blood seemed to freeze.
>
> "You mentioned Ravensbruck in your talk," he was saying. "I was a guard in there." No, he did not remember me.
>
> "But since that time," he went on, "I have become a Christian. I know that God has forgiven me for the cruel things I did there, but I would like to hear it from your lips as well. Fräulein,"—again the hand came out—"will you forgive me?"
>
> And I stood there—I whose sins had again and again been forgiven—and could not forgive. Betsie [her sister] had died in that place—could he erase her slow terrible death simply for the asking?
>
> It could not have been many seconds that he stood there, hand held out, but to me it seemed hours as I wrestled with the most difficult thing I had ever had to do.
>
> For I had to do it—I knew that. The message that God forgives has a prior condition: that we forgive those who have injured us. "If you do not forgive men their trespasses,"

Jesus says, "neither will your Father in heaven forgive your trespasses."

I knew it not only as a commandment of God, but as a daily experience. Since the end of the war, I had had a home in Holland for victims of Nazi brutality. Those who were able to forgive their former enemies were able to return to the outside world and rebuild their lives, no matter what the physical scars. Those who nursed their bitterness remained invalids. It was as simple and as horrible as that.

And still I stood there with the coldness clutching my heart. But forgiveness is not an emotion—I knew that too. Forgiveness is an act of the will, and the will can function regardless of the temperature of the heart. *Jesus, help me!* I prayed silently. *I can lift my hand. I can do that much. You supply the feeling.*

And so woodenly, mechanically, I thrust my hand into the one stretched out to me. And as I did, an incredible thing took place. The current started in my shoulder, raced down my arm, sprang into our joined hands. And then this healing warmth seemed to flood my whole being, bringing tears to my eyes. "I forgive you, brother!" I cried. "With all my heart!"

For a long moment we grasped each other's hands, the former guard and the former prisoner. I had never known God's love so intensely as I did then.[11]

This is a powerful and deeply moving example of what a struggle it can be to offer forgiveness even to a repentant person.

Nor is repentance easy! Even at the level of ordinary life, most of us find it difficult even to say we are sorry, let alone really to admit to ourselves that we are wrong and repent at the deepest level. Some of us find it hard to say we are sorry to our spouse and apologize to our children, don't we?

Indeed, it can be a sobering test question to ask ourselves: When was the last time we said "I'm sorry" to someone, or apologized for

---

11. Corrie ten Boom (with Jamie Buckingham), *Tramp for the Lord: The Story That Begins Where the Hiding Ends* (Fort Washington, PA: CLC Publications, 1974), 56–57.

something we had done and asked for forgiveness? The Lord's Prayer says we need two things: daily food and forgiveness. We would notice it if we missed our daily meals. What about forgiveness?

To sum up: suppose that I have been wronged in some way, hurt or offended, and am faced with the question of forgiving the one who hurt me. I have two things to think about, one inward and the other outward. The first is to get to the stage where I can prevent the wrong from damaging me by letting it go inwardly. This involves being prepared to let it go outwardly when appropriate. And when is that? When the offender repents. Then I must (as a Christian, certainly) let it go publicly so that the repentant wrongdoer knows that I have forgiven him.

Language is a problem here. When the word *forgive* is used, most people at once think of a public and outer forgiveness, not a private letting go and willingness to forgive. We really need a word other than *forgive* for the latter, but we don't have one, so the confusion remains.

This all leaves the question of how we are to understand the unforgettable response of Gordon Wilson, who was so magnanimous in his attitude to those who murdered his daughter, or the response of the Amish community to the shooting of their children. In light of what we have said, are such responses, where there is no apparent demand or even request for repentance, really to be taken as letting the offenders off the hook and essentially condoning the offenses?

I cannot imagine this to be the case, although some critics thought it did. What I think may be happening is that many, if not most, people are unaware of the two meanings of forgiveness so that when they offer what appears to be an unconditional public "letting it go," what they are really declaring is not that the offense does not matter, but that they have inwardly let it go and are not harboring an unforgiving spirit or looking for vengeance.

Recall what the Amish scholars said: "The Amish willingness to forgo vengeance does not undo the tragedy or pardon the wrong, but rather constitutes a first step toward a future that is more hopeful." The Amish used the word *forgive* in the context of the shooting, but it would seem that their concept of forgiveness does not necessarily include pardon, letting go of the offense to the offender publicly.

Gordon Wilson's words, "I bear them no ill-will, I bear them no grudge," were interpreted as forgiveness by the media. And so they were, but in what sense? Certainly those words were a rare example of inner releasing and outer refusal to take vengeance, and they display real willingness to forgive.

With all these things in mind we return to Joseph. He clearly thought that there could never be complete forgiveness and reconciliation unless his brothers acted consistently with their claim to be honest men and repented. The narrative tells us how Joseph used his ability and power to give them the opportunity to do just that.

According to Genesis, a higher hand than that of Joseph was also involved. God was responsible for sending the famine that brought Joseph's brothers down to Egypt. This means that to get the men to repent and be reconciled to one another, God himself intervened in the natural cycle of things. And in case you think that is extraordinary or extreme—that repentance, forgiveness, and reconciliation are surely not that important—how will you respond to the fact that to give you and me the opportunity to repent and experience his forgiveness, God himself became human and visited planet earth?

The sheer importance of this matter of forgiveness in God's eyes is shown by the fact that it is the principal topic in eight chapters, Genesis 42–50, whereas the description of creation takes up just two. We have seen that the process of bringing the brothers to repentance has already started in that they admit their guilt to one another, not knowing that Joseph could understand what they were saying. It was this that precipitated Joseph's weeping, and the fact that he did so near the start of this part of the narrative shows that thoughts of forgiveness were already in his heart and mind. How would he take the matter forward?

Joseph gathered from overhearing the brothers' conversation that the eldest, Reuben, had tried to protect him, something he hadn't known before, although he may well have wryly thought, "Good thing that Reuben did not succeed, or I might well be dead." Still, Reuben had tried, and, maybe for that reason, Joseph chose Simeon, the second-oldest brother, to be his hostage and bound him before their eyes. Another reason for choosing Simeon may have been that he was the ringleader in the gratuitous violence perpetrated against the men of Shechem. Perhaps Joseph even suspected him of being the ringleader in attempting to kill Joseph himself. Joseph then told his servants to fill all the remaining brothers' sacks with grain, together with the silver they had paid for it.

It is hard to imagine the mood among the group of men as they left for home knowing that they would have to tell Jacob that they had been forced to leave Simeon behind and that the governor of Egypt had insisted that they return with Benjamin in order for matters to be sorted out. They halted for the night, and one of them noticed that his silver money was in the mouth of his sack. Their hearts sank, and they began to tremble and said, "What is this that God has done to us?" (42:28). They were shaken to the core and began dimly to perceive that God was speaking to them. He was, though it was Joseph who had played a trick on them. Years before they had received silver for Joseph; now they were receiving silver from Joseph, though they did not know it.

So they came to their father and told him what had happened. It must have been confusing for Jacob to hear, on the one hand, of Joseph's special concern for the youngest son, and yet, on the other hand, his harshness in dealing with Simeon. The brothers then emptied their sacks and discovered that all of them had had their silver returned, and not just the one who discovered his at the stopping place. They were terrified. That mass of glittering silver could not fail to have triggered the memory of the silver for which they had sold Joseph.

If so, Jacob broke into that memory, saying: "You have bereaved me of my children" (42:36). Over the years his suspicion had grown that his sons had robbed him of Joseph. "Joseph is no more, Simeon is no more, and now you would take Benjamin. All this has come against me" (42:36). Jacob feels that he is losing his family one by one. He is full of self-pity, which is shown by exaggeration. Yes, Joseph was no more (so far as Jacob knew), but Simeon was still alive, and no one wanted to take Benjamin in any absolute and permanent sense. Jacob thinks that everything is directed against him.

Self-pity, especially in those who are older, can so easily turn into bitterness or worse. C. S. Lewis put it this way: "The moment you have a self at all, there is a possibility of putting yourself first, wanting to be the centre, wanting to be God, in fact. That was the sin of Satan: and that was the sin he taught the human race."[12]

One of the best antidotes to self-pity when we feel it creeping up on us is to count our many blessings and name them one by one, as the old hymn, "Count Your Many Blessings," says.[13] That will give us reason to be thankful, and self-pity cannot easily coexist with gratitude, especially with gratitude to God.

What is also sad is that Jacob clearly has no awareness, or none that he would admit, that he is largely responsible for the situation by his favoritism for Joseph that inevitably stirred up hatred on the part of the rest of his sons.

How Reuben felt about that, we can only guess, for he next makes an extraordinarily foolish and intemperate suggestion: "Kill my two sons if I do not bring him back to you" (42:37). We have already seen evidence of Reuben's instability, but this goes beyond all sense. Jacob has just been accusing them of depriving him of his children, and Reuben says, "Well, if I don't sort it out,

---

12. C. S. Lewis, *Mere Christianity* (New York: Macmillan, 1952), 53.
13. Johnson Oatman Jr., "Count Your Many Blessings," 1897.

you can kill two more." That would then leave even more gaps in the family; it would sacrifice the future generation for the sake of the present. It made no moral or practical sense whatsoever.

Reuben's conscience had been niggling at him for years because of the things he had done. He had tried to rescue Joseph by having him put in the pit. But then he hadn't followed through to protect Joseph when the others sold him to the slave traders. He had kept silent when the lie about Joseph's death was told to Jacob. He had kept silent for years, a silence that had deeply troubled his conscience and poisoned his life.

"Put him in my hands, and I will bring him back to you," Reuben continued (42:37). No way was Jacob going to agree: "My son shall not go down with you, for his brother is dead, and he is the only one left" (42:38). There was only one other son of Jacob's favorite wife to remind him of Joseph. And Jacob was not prepared to let him out of his sight. But what an insensitive thing to say to Reuben, or indeed any of his sons. Reuben was left, and the other sons apart from Simeon were still with Jacob. What was Reuben to think as Jacob once more paraded his favoritism for Joseph?

The family had reached an impasse. They could not go back to Egypt with any hope of Simeon being released unless Benjamin was with them. Jacob decisively blocked that, clearly prepared for the family to go on as usual without Simeon. In this instance, the man full of self-pity did what such people often do—shut out reality by sticking his head firmly in the sand. That is, in Jacob's case, until God pulls it out again.

17

The Path of Forgiveness and Reconciliation, Act 2

The ongoing stalemate was broken by the most elemental of things—hunger. The famine got steadily worse, and the supplies that the brothers had brought from Egypt had run out. Jacob needed food for himself and his family, so he suggested that the brothers go to buy some.

Judah stepped up as the spokesman for the brothers and reminded Jacob that they had been solemnly warned not to return without their brother Benjamin. Jacob, as was often the case, reacted with self-pity; why had they told "the man" that they had another brother? Judah parried this by pointing out that the man had shown great interest in the family, and how, in any case, were they to know he would ask them to bring their other brother to Egypt?

Judah then, pointing out that the family would die out if they did not get food, asked his father to send Benjamin with him. The very future survival of the family was at stake and that was far more important than Jacob maintaining his protective attitude toward the adult Benjamin.

Judah then offered himself as a pledge of Benjamin's safety: "If *I* do not bring him back to you and set him before you, then

186 Joseph, His Father, and His Brothers

let *me* bear the blame forever" (Gen. 43:9). The fact that Joseph was his brother had meant nothing to Judah when he instigated selling him to the Ishmaelites. But Judah had undergone a radical change of heart so that now he personally guaranteed to protect Benjamin for his father's sake.

The mention of the pledge reminds us that Judah had himself lost two sons and, showing no interest in the preservation of his own family line, had failed to give his widowed daughter-in-law Tamar in marriage to his third son. Tamar, desperate for a family, deceived Judah into sleeping with her but cleverly asked a pledge that identified him as the father of her child. Now it was not his staff Judah was offering as a pledge, but himself. Reuben had not offered himself, but his sons.

Judah was prepared to act as a substitute for Benjamin. This was a huge step forward for Judah in terms of character and maturity. In earlier years when plotting to rid the family of Joseph, he had not cared at all for how his father might react to the loss of a son. By this point Judah was beginning to care and to take real and possibly costly responsibility to see that it did not happen again. It was a big move, a move that took him closer to repentance. It could also be read as a move closer to the leadership of the clan, Reuben having failed. Perhaps it is best understood as both.

Judah finally told Jacob bluntly that they needed to get on with it: if they had acted earlier they could already have been to Egypt and back twice.

Jacob, seeing no other option, caved in. He instructed his sons to take a present for "the man," balm, a little honey, gum, myrrh, pistachio nuts, and almonds. This strikes me as almost comical, as if such a tiny present is going to make any difference to the governor of Egypt, second only to Pharaoh. "Take double the money with you," adds Jacob. "Carry back with you the money that was returned in the mouth of your sacks. Perhaps it was an oversight. Take also your brother, and arise, go again to the man" (43:12–13). Jacob finally commited them to God: "May God

Almighty grant you mercy before the man, and may he send back your other brother and Benjamin. And as for me, if I am bereaved of my children, I am bereaved" (43:14).

Jacob feared the worst and had resigned himself to it. One cannot help feeling sorry for him. He had entrusted his youngest son, his last connection with his beloved wife Rachel, to sons whom he suspected of responsibility for Joseph's death. They were on the way to meet what Jacob imagined to be an unpredictable Egyptian overlord who had already taken Simeon captive. Jacob, not for the first time in his life, was utterly alone and could only wait.

Meanwhile, the brothers found themselves standing before Joseph once more. Joseph saw Benjamin with them and immediately ordered his steward to take them to his house and prepare dinner for them. This ratcheted up the brothers' fear, and they at first suspected that Joseph wished to assault them and seize them and their donkeys because of the money that was replaced in their sacks. It is unclear by what logic they could have reached that conclusion apart from the sense that they were being toyed with for some unknown reason.

They decide to speak to Joseph's steward about the money, and the steward disturbed them even more by responding, "Peace to you, do not be afraid. Your God and the God of your fathers has put treasure in your sacks for you. I received your money" (43:23).

The steward attributed to God the actions ordered by Joseph. What could an Egyptian steward know of their God and the God of their fathers—unless he had come under some Hebrew influence? Presumably, Joseph had told him what to say, and maybe Joseph was not being disingenuous, as many suggest, but had a real sense in his heart that God was prompting his actions all along.

Simeon was then brought out and reunited with his brothers, and the steward very courteously took them into Joseph's house, a palatial building, no doubt, and washed their feet in oriental fashion and fed their pack animals, while they got their little present ready for Joseph's arrival. They had feared assault, yet they were being treated as honored guests. It was disconcerting, to say the least.

Joseph arrived, and they gave him the present and bowed down to the ground before him. He inquired about their father and they said: "Your servant our father is well; he is still alive" (43:28). They bowed again, prostrate on the ground. Now all eleven sheaves were bowing, and Joseph must have been overwhelmed with a sense of fulfillment. How many years he had hoped for this moment, and it had arrived.

He looked up, and his attention was caught by Benjamin, his only full sibling. Still addressing all of them he said, "Is this your youngest brother, of whom you spoke to me? God be gracious to you, my son!" (43:29). It must have sounded extraordinary to them. What was going on? At that point Joseph, deeply moved by the sight of his brother, could no longer control himself and rushed out to a private room and wept.

Why did Joseph not just throw his arms around Benjamin and tell them all who he was? He clearly did not think that the time was yet ripe for disclosure. His compassion at this point was for Benjamin, not the others. Benjamin had not been involved in their wickedness. Joseph needed to be certain that they had really repented, and as yet he had little evidence of that. The story had not yet reached its climax.

He washed his face, composed himself, came out, and ordered the food served. He sat alone, as Egyptian custom dictated, and they sat at a separate table and were amazed as it slowly dawned on them that they were seated in the exact order of their ages. Now these were grown men, born in fairly rapid succession, and it would have been impossible for a stranger to guess their ages accurately, and the probability of getting it right by chance is negligible. It was uncanny. The seating arrangement was obviously a result of intelligent design; a higher hand was at work. What could it possibly mean?

Then another odd thing happened. Food was carried from Joseph's table to theirs, and Benjamin was unaccountably given five times as much as anyone else. They drank and made merry together, though a nervous merriment.

Joseph then made ready for the final test to prove the honesty of his brothers and to give them the opportunity to repent. He ordered his steward to fill the men's sacks with grain and to put their money back in the sacks and a special silver goblet belonging to Joseph into Benjamin's sack.

18

The Path of Forgiveness and Reconciliation, Act 3

The next day at dawn the eleven brothers, united again, started the long journey home, no doubt massively relieved at the success of their mission. However, they had not gone far when, at Joseph's order, his steward overtook them and accused them of stealing the valuable goblet. They were stunned and pointed out that they had returned all the money found in their sacks after the first visit, so why should they steal anything? Knowing they have to suggest something, they proposed that whoever was found with the goblet should die, and the rest should become slaves—a wild, impulsive suggestion.

But Joseph had other ideas. Acting for him, his steward proposed something more appropriate: "He who is found with it shall be my servant, and the rest of you shall be innocent" (Gen. 44:10). The search commenced with the eldest and ended with the discovery of the goblet in Benjamin's sack.

What would they now do? The choice was momentous. Would they leave Benjamin, as they had left Joseph years before, and go home without him? They had an opportunity here to be rid not only of Joseph but of Benjamin and to put an end to their father's hated policy of favoritism. Or had they gone so far in their repentance for what they had done to Joseph that they would stick with Benjamin, come what may?

Robert Sacks gets it exactly right when he says: "Joseph has now decided to put his brothers to the final test. He will place them in a position where they will be strongly tempted to treat Benjamin as they had treated him. The point of Joseph's trial is that repentance is only complete when one knows that if he were placed in the same position he would not act in the way he had acted before."[1]

The brothers make their great decision that, come what may, they would not abandon Benjamin as they had Joseph long before. They tore their clothes as a sign of despair and mourning (over Benjamin or self-pity?) and returned with the steward to the city. Their ordeal was not over yet. But they had made the right decision. They would stand, all of them, with their brother Benjamin.

Then, for the final time, they were brought before Joseph the governor, who was waiting for them in his house. Once more they prostrated themselves on the ground before him and Joseph faced them: "What deed is this that you have done? Do you not know that a man like me can indeed practice divination?" (44:15). Presumably this was said to scare them even further and raise the stakes, rather than its being a confession that he did actually practice divination, which would be completely out of character with his core beliefs and for which there is no evidence. In addition, he had no need to do so. Furthermore, the cup was part of an elaborate setup. Kitchen comments:

> A two-tablet "handbook" for divining from patterns of oil on water in a cup comes from the Old Babylonian period (early second millennium), while a pair of small statuettes from Egypt of seemingly Middle Kingdom date may show

---

1. Cited in Leon Kass, *The Beginning of Wisdom: Reading Genesis* (New York: Free Press, 2003), 591.

the process, otherwise known only from demotic texts of the second century A.D.[2]

Judah, acting as leader for the group, spoke up and confessed their collective guilt, saying that God had found it out (not Joseph!). Judah appeared increasingly aware of God's involvement in the drama. "We are my lord's servants," he said (44:16).

Joseph then faced them for the second time with the crucial choice: "Only the man in whose hand the cup was found shall be my servant. But as for you, go up in peace to your father" (44:17). There would be no collective punishment. Only the guilty Benjamin would stay.

What must Benjamin have thought? He knew he was not guilty, so why was Joseph being so rough on him? He must have guessed that the whole thing had been engineered by the Egyptians. But why? That was the puzzle.

This was crunch time. The band of brothers was once more free to go. Would they? Would they, under pressure, abandon Benjamin to slavery, just as once they had abandoned Joseph to slavery? The past was rising up to face them. Some have suggested that Joseph would have been glad to retain Benjamin in Egypt and let the brothers go and have Jacob die. But this is hardly likely in view of the scheme Joseph had in mind to replicate the past, as indicated in the way the story eventually turns out.

Judah then steps up and embarks on one of the greatest and most moving speeches in all literature. It is the longest speech in the book of Genesis. In it he proves his worthiness to be the leader of the tribe; in it he shows a superior ability to move hearts and minds as he pleads with the governor of Egypt for the life of his brother. Showing great, almost obsequious, deference, he asks permission to speak to one who is "like Pharaoh himself" (44:18) and asks him not to be angry, subtly hinting that, in Judah's view, he has been angry in the past. He rehearsed

---

2. K. A. Kitchen, *On the Reliability of the Old Testament* (Grand Rapids, MI: Eerdmans, 2006), 351.

what had happened so far: their first visit, when they were asked about their family and told of Jacob their father at home with his youngest son, whom, Judah added for the first time, he loves. He reminded the august governor of Egypt that it was he who said they must bring their youngest brother with them or they would get no further audience with him. He is the one who has forced this situation on them.

Judah then told what his father Jacob had said when they got home and informed him of this request: "You know that my wife bore me two sons. One left me, and I said, 'Surely he has been torn to pieces,' and I have never seen him since. If you take this one also from me, and harm happens to him, you will bring down my gray hairs in evil to Sheol" (44:27–29).

Judah wanted the governor to see the narrative through Jacob's eyes. He wanted him to feel Jacob's emotional distress at losing his son, so he stressed what both Joseph and Benjamin meant to Jacob. We notice that Judah concentrated on Rachel's two children and did not mention his other brothers. This conveys a picture of Jacob as an old man rather pathetically doting on the one child he has left from that union and desperate to protect him from harm. The subtext is that it would be Joseph and no one else bringing this disaster on the family.

It is hard to imagine that Joseph, listening to this, and recalling his father's care for him as a boy, could fail to be moved by both its content and the fact that Judah was saying it, the very brother who had sold him into slavery without a thought about what it would mean to their father. Nor could he fail to see the burden of pain he had felt necessary to lay on his brothers to get them to this place. This was a transformed Judah speaking. Something had happened in the man's heart that was bringing him ever nearer to repentance. And Judah had more to say:

Now therefore, as soon as I come to your servant my father, and the boy is not with us, then, as his life is bound up in the boy's life, as soon as he sees that the boy is not with us, he will die, and your servants will bring down the gray hairs of your servant our father with sorrow to Sheol. For your servant became a pledge of safety for the boy to my father, saying, "If I do not bring him back to you, then I shall bear the blame before my father all my life." (44:30–32)

Joseph's heart churned as he heard that Judah had pledged himself to bring Benjamin home to his father and was prepared to bear the blame for failing to do so. Judah then launched the final arrow that pierced Joseph's heart: "Now therefore, please let your servant remain instead of the boy as a servant to my lord, and let the boy go back with his brothers. For how can I go back to my father if the boy is not with me? I fear to see the evil that would find my father" (44:33–34).

"Please, please," he begs, "take me instead of Benjamin. I cannot go back home without him. I fear for what would happen to my father." Judah, who had spent years not fearing his father's response to the "death" of Joseph, had come to see the love his father had for his son and offered himself as a substitute. The last word he addressed to Joseph was *avi*, "my father." Its resonance could no longer be resisted.

The test was over. Real repentance had been reached and therefore genuine forgiveness could be offered. Joseph ordered all his retainers and servants to leave. Joseph's tears poured down his face to the amazement of the men that watched in astonished fascination and concern. He had wept twice before, but here they saw it for the first time. He wept aloud with such exceptional intensity and lack of restraint that the sound carried far beyond the room, and the Egyptians heard it. He spoke, and to their total surprise the brothers heard him address them in their own language with the stunningly unexpected words: "I am Joseph! Is my father still alive?" (45:3).

They shrank back in terror. "So Joseph said to his brothers, 'Come near to me, please.' And they came near. And he said, 'I am your brother, Joseph, whom you sold into Egypt'" (45:4). That statement cleared away any lingering doubt, if there was one, that the speaker was Joseph. How would anyone else have known that he had been sold as a slave? Joseph continued with reassurance:

> And now do not be distressed or angry with yourselves because you sold me here, for God sent me before you to preserve life. For the famine has been in the land these two years, and there are yet five years in which there will be neither plowing nor harvest. And God sent me before you to preserve for you a remnant on earth, and to keep alive for you many survivors. So it was not you who sent me here, but God. He has made me a father to Pharaoh, and lord of all his house and ruler over all the land of Egypt. (45:5–8)

Joseph sought immediately to put his brothers at ease about the matter that was uppermost in their minds—this was the Joseph that they had sold into slavery to get him out of their lives, and they were completely at his mercy.

Joseph stated the fact of their deed but then at once encouraged them not to be distressed since it was God who providentially had sent Joseph to Egypt to preserve life in the midst of a famine that would run for a further five years. Joseph stressed God's initiative in the whole business, saying that it was not, in the end, the brothers who sent him to Egypt, but God. This double causation is important in connection with the biblical view of the relationship between God's sovereignty and human responsibility. This, as the countless words written about it testify, is a very deep matter. Joseph seems to understand that although ultimately the hand behind it all was God's, his brothers were responsible for what they had done—otherwise Joseph's testing of whether their repentance was genuine could be taken as a charade. If the brothers were simply puppets on strings manipulated by God, then one could no more think of their guilt than the guilt of a robot.[3]

---

3. See my *Determined to Believe?: The Sovereignty of God, Freedom, Faith, and Human Responsibility* (Oxford, UK: Lion Hudson, 2017).

Joseph's was, by any account, a magnanimous, forgiving speech calculated to assuage their guilt, fear, and pain and to achieve reconciliation. He told them that they should not be angry with themselves. He was aware that the burden of their exposed guilt could lead to a very unhealthy "we cannot forgive ourselves" kind of attitude, a matter to which we shall return. Here, we gain the impression that Joseph was actually beginning to love his brothers.

Joseph had a clear sense that God had been active behind the scenes in his providential care and faithfulness to his promise. Yet his brothers were now aware that the dreams they resented had come true, and Joseph was in an exalted position, not only over them but over the whole empire.

Before we move on with the narrative, it is important that we reflect on the role of Judah in this life-changing drama. At the heart of his success lies Judah's willingness to become a substitute for his brother in order for that brother to return to his father. There is something noble and magnificent about this, and we would be sorely lacking in imagination if we fail to see here the contours of something infinitely bigger that involves not Judah personally, who never actually became a substitute, but his descendant, that great Lion of the tribe of Judah, the promised seed, the Messiah, Jesus Christ our Lord, who did give himself as a perfect substitute in dying for sinful men and women so that they could be reconciled to the Father. In other words, there are deep pointers to the gospel of Jesus Christ embedded in the Joseph narrative. That is early evidence that substitution lies at the heart of forgiveness and reconciliation, and that evidence will be augmented by the imagery of the Passover and the offerings associated with both tabernacle and temple as history moves from such shadows and pointers toward the actual atonement Christ made on the cross.

Returning to the text we see that Joseph's primary concern was now with his father. His instructions to his brothers were unequivocal and show that Joseph had no intention of returning to the simple life he had once known in Canaan:

Hurry and go up to my father and say to him, "Thus says your son Joseph, God has made me lord of all Egypt. Come down to me; do not tarry. You shall dwell in the land of Goshen, and you shall be near me, you and your children and your children's children, and your flocks, your herds, and all that you have. There I will provide for you, for there are yet five years of famine to come, so that you and your household, and all that you have, do not come to poverty." (45:9–11)

Go to *my* father, not *our* father. Was there more than a tinge of regret in Joseph's mind that he had failed to communicate with his father in the preceding seven years during which he had had the means to do so? Of course, it is easy to say that if he had, then the brothers would have heard of it, and the events we have just been considering would not have happened. It may be that Joseph was so convinced that his boyhood dreams would come true that he felt an inner constraint not to do anything about it until God showed his hand, experience having taught him the importance of waiting on God.

Joseph's message revealed that he wanted to ensure that his father realized that Joseph had become a man of great power and prestige, a fact that may well help corroborate in Jacob's mind that this was indeed Joseph, the son who dreamed that his father would one day bow to him. It also set the context for Joseph telling his father to come to him. Jacob would surely understand that the second in command of the Egyptian empire could not simply abdicate his responsibility and rush off into obscurity, especially since there were still five more years of famine for which Joseph's administrative ability was essential.

Joseph therefore commanded his family to come down to Egypt so that he could provide for them and shield them from starvation and extinction. He was not aware that this move would eventually lead to four centuries of subjugation and slavery of Israel in Egypt. There would be plenty of horror to come. Joseph was still speaking:

"And now your eyes see, and the eyes of my brother Benjamin see, that it is my mouth that speaks to you. You must tell my father of all my honor in Egypt, and of all that you have seen. Hurry and bring my father down here." Then he fell upon his brother Benjamin's neck and wept, and Benjamin wept upon his neck. And he kissed all his brothers and wept upon them. After that his brothers talked with him. (45:12–15)

If there was any residual doubt in the brothers' minds as to Joseph's identity, it disappeared as Joseph used his brother Benjamin's name for the first time in his hearing. No one but Joseph would have known it. Joseph, speaking to all of them, called Benjamin *my* brother, thus maintaining, whether consciously or not, a distance between them. He had forgiven their wrongdoing, but consequences inevitably remained.

Joseph wept with Benjamin, and Benjamin wept with him as years of pent-up feelings found release in an intense catharsis. Rachel's sons had found each other again, and great was their joy. They would have a great deal to catch up on in the days to come.

Joseph also wept over his brothers, but it is not said that they wept with him. We are simply told that there was a great deal of conversation about which we are given no further detail. Yet even this brief record leaves us with the feeling that the ten brothers were still wary of Joseph and would be for some time to come.

19

Israel Comes to Egypt

The story reached the ears of Pharaoh, and he showed himself magnanimous, instructing Joseph to offer his father and family the very best of the land in Egypt. Presumably Pharaoh was more than grateful for Joseph's economic wonder, which was in process of saving the empire from starvation, to say nothing of helping Pharaoh retain his own power base. At Pharaoh's command, Joseph ordered wagons to provide transport for all of Jacob's family and retinue and sent his brothers back to Canaan with a warning not to quarrel on the way. Joseph had no illusions regarding them; their journey was not yet over. Nor was that of the nation of Israel, which would spring from Jacob's family. Joseph did not realize that the generosity flowing from Egypt to his family would one day result in a four-hundred-year slavery from which the nation of Israel would one day have to be delivered. All that future hardship was veiled from them, but the decision that would lead to it was made that day.

There are subtle differences between what the two rulers of Egypt, Joseph and Pharaoh, offered to Jacob's family. Both asked them, indeed, commanded them to come down to Egypt, but Joseph suggested that they come and live separated from the

Egyptians by forming an enclave in the district of Goshen in the fertile eastern Nile Delta. Pharaoh, by contrast, repeatedly offered them the best of the land of Egypt. Joseph urged his father to come with all his flocks and possessions, whereas Pharaoh told them to leave all their stuff behind and not to regret it.

These differences raise a very important question: would Israel be assimilated completely into Egypt and lose all its distinctiveness, as Pharaoh seems to wish, or can the Seed Project, the vision of Abraham, be preserved by Israel's keeping its cultural identity, living as a nation within a nation? Assimilation versus separation is an issue that has already raised its head in Genesis and will recur throughout the entire history of Israel.

Pharaoh may well have imagined that Joseph had himself been completely assimilated and therefore so too should his family. Perhaps that tension is reflected in the fact that there are two distinct descriptions of Jacob's sons in this text. They are called both "Joseph's brothers" and "the sons of Israel." What is clear is that Pharaoh had different ideas from Joseph, and so eventually would one of his successors who "did not know Joseph" (Ex. 1:8).

They were soon sent on their journey with ample provisions, though here once more Joseph differentiated between Benjamin and the others by giving him five changes of clothes and three hundred pieces of silver. It is almost as if he was returning to Benjamin the clothes that had once been torn from him and giving him silver in return for the silver the other brothers had obtained for Joseph. Joseph was favoring Benjamin as once his father had favored him—with what ultimate consequence, we may well wonder.

Not surprisingly Jacob was stunned when he got the news that Joseph was alive and was ruler of Egypt. At first he did not believe it: "his heart became numb" (Gen. 45:26). We can imagine that the man was at risk of a heart attack. Judah had warned that the loss of Benjamin would kill the old man; the knowledge that Joseph was still alive nearly did. It was a heart-stopping shock.

However, when the brothers reported what Joseph had said, and when Jacob saw the tangible evidence of wealth in the wagons standing in his courtyard, he rapidly came back to life and decided to go and see his long-lost son before he died. He would once more be a father to and for his son.

On his journey Jacob stopped at Beersheva, a place that was of great significance to him and his family. It was where his grandfather Abraham had gone after the drama of binding his son Isaac. It was there that God had appeared to Isaac, and it was from there that Jacob had set out on his travels years before. So Jacob stopped and offered a sacrifice to God. And God broke his silence of twenty-two years and spoke to Jacob for the first time since Joseph was a boy. The language, as Jacob probably knew, was similar to that used in God's speech to Abraham when he told him to offer up his son Isaac. God called to him in a vision of the night:

> And God spoke to Israel in visions of the night and said, "Jacob, Jacob." And he said, "Here I am." Then he said, "I am God, the God of your father. Do not be afraid to go down to Egypt, for there I will make you into a great nation. I myself will go down with you to Egypt, and I will also bring you up again, and Joseph's hand shall close your eyes." (46:2–4)

It was a momentous move that Jacob was about to take, as historically important as Abraham's departure from Ur of the Chaldeans to travel to the Promised Land. And in light of the subsequent history of Israel in Egypt, as described in the book of Exodus, what God said to Jacob is remarkable. It seems calculated to reassure Jacob about his immediate next step: he should not fear to take Joseph's advice and move to Egypt, for there the Seed Project of making Israel a great nation would be realized. The fact that this would happen in Egypt is a new part of the biblical revelation.

There is no hint that Joseph feared that the nation would be assimilated into Egypt and lose its cultural identity. Neither is there any indication of the fact that such assimilation would be avoided by Israel becoming a nation of slaves to subsequent pharaohs. God simply promised that he would go down with Jacob to Egypt and bring him up again and that Joseph would be with him when he died. Did God mean bring him back to Canaan in a coffin, or did he mean eventually bring the nation back under Moses?

Jacob must have known what God had said to his grandfather Abraham when he made the covenant with Abraham regarding his posterity:

> Then the LORD said to Abram, "Know for certain that your offspring will be sojourners in a land that is not theirs and will be servants there, and they will be afflicted for four hundred years. But I will bring judgment on the nation that they serve, and afterward they shall come out with great possessions. As for you, you shall go to your fathers in peace; you shall be buried in a good old age. And they shall come back here in the fourth generation, for the iniquity of the Amorites is not yet complete." (15:13–16)

God's message to Abraham concerned the distant future, and Jacob was surely aware of every detail of the making of the covenant, including this prediction that Abraham's, and therefore Jacob's, descendants would go to a foreign land and suffer four hundred years' affliction. And here Jacob was about to make such a move, and God was encouraging him to make it without explicitly reminding him of the darkly foreboding prediction of suffering that it entailed. Joseph also must have heard in his childhood the detail of God's covenant with Abraham as central to the family's great calling. Yet there is no hint in the narrative that he had any recollection of it.

And even if they had thought of it, what difference would or could it have made? Maybe these thoughts were somewhere in the back of Jacob's mind. Whatever the answer, God did not leave him any option in the matter: he told him to go down. But God did not tell him everything. Also, such specific guidance appears to be very rare. Indeed, we notice the same phenomenon in the life of the apostle Paul, as recorded in Acts. Only seldom does God speak directly to him.

We might well ask, we who are neither Jacob nor Paul, what principle there is to be found here that might apply to us. There is at least one right on the surface. The guidance in these rare incidents is usually concerned with what to do or what will happen and is special because a historic turning point has been reached. Here, Israel was to go to Egypt, and in Acts, Paul was to go to Europe.

However, it is easy to make the mistake of thinking that guidance has solely to do with action, with what we do, and therefore to make the second mistake of thinking that there is no guidance at other times. God is just as concerned, probably more concerned, with who we are and certainly most concerned with our relationship with him, for which we were created. Experiencing that fellowship is not a rare thing but is rather an ongoing reality supported by prayer and feeding on the Scriptures and the sense of the Holy Spirit within, without the need for any special voices or visions of the night. God expects us in the main to get our help from these sources in the context of developing our relationship with him so that when we have to make a decision, the guidance we receive consists of all the accumulated experience of God we have had up to that moment, plus our conscious commitment of the matter to him.

We should not doubt that God will help and support us, his Spirit within us, but he will not (usually) make the decision for us. The reason for that is surely very plain. When our children are small, they look to us as parents for almost every decision. However, if this is still the situation in their twenties, it is sad since it indicates that they have not matured. Character is developed through the decisions we make, and God wants us to grow up to be his mature sons and daughters. Therefore, we must be wary of a subtle tendency to expect God to decide everything for us.

The fundamental Christian confession is "Jesus Christ is Lord," not, "He wants to be Lord," or, "He should be Lord." We may assume that he is guiding us in life; we don't have to persuade him since he is more interested in our life than we are. It follows that if we make what turns out to be a false step, we can trust him to continue to guide us and bring us to see the right thing to do.

This makes all of life an experience of God's gracious guidance, not just those rare special moments of specific course correction. It is important to realize that Joseph, who experienced God being with him, did not, so far as we know, have any special experience, unlike Jacob, of God speaking to him.

And so, at God's behest, Israel took the first step toward Egypt, and history began to move toward the first diaspora, a scattering of the seed on which the success of the Seed Project depends. Genesis gives us a formal list of the names of the seventy people (the sixty-six who came with Jacob plus Joseph and his children who were already there) that constituted the family of Israel in Egypt.

Judah, not surprisingly, had been chosen as the leader of the caravan to guide the clan to the Goshen district of Egypt. It is noteworthy that Jacob did not go directly to seek out either Joseph or Pharaoh but went to the part of Egypt that Joseph had indicated would be suitable for the family to settle. There he waited for Joseph to come to him.

Joseph prepared his chariots and presented himself to Jacob. The terminology depicting this is unusual, as elsewhere in Scripture it is used in connection with God appearing to someone. Joseph in his Egyptian regalia with his wagons and retinue may well have appeared godlike, certainly to his subjects.

Despite his regal appearance, Joseph fell on Jacob's neck and wept a good while. We are not told that Jacob wept, which means that he probably didn't but stood dry-eyed and bewildered. Jacob may well have been wary as he tried to process this development that he thought he would never see. On the one hand, he knew that Joseph was still alive. But Joseph had changed beyond recognition. He looked like an Egyptian, spoke the language of Egypt, and was chief minister in the country's administration. He had an Egyptian wife from the highest priestly order of an Egyptian polytheistic religion as far removed from Israel's monotheism as it could be.

Although he had his son back physically, Jacob must have wondered whether his son had been lost to the Seed Project by his assimilation into a heathen culture. What, too, of his other sons? For now Jacob knew (although he had probably long suspected) that they had lied to him about the death of Joseph. Not only that, but they had sustained the lie for over twenty years. What was he to think? What was he to do? It was devastating. It is striking that there is no record of the sons' expressing repentance to Jacob for what they had done.

Jacob's concern is understandable. In the contemporary world also, many believers now in middle age have lived to see the culture around them change completely in terms of its values and norms and attitudes to faith in God and Christ. They cannot help noticing the effects of secularization on their children and the rapidity with which the Christian teaching they received at home disappears. Relationships from a family perspective may remain good, and we should thank God for that, but the question that troubles many parents is, *Are their children still committed to the great project of the kingdom of God as they once appeared to be?*

The warnings in the New Testament of the dangers of falling in love with the world were not made lightly, and each of us needs to take real care not to to be seduced by an incremental assimilation that lands us in the joylessness of compromise.

And what do we do when we find that some of our children or friends have lied to us? There are no easy answers here.

Joseph's immediate concern was to establish good relationships between his family and Pharaoh in such a way that Israel could retain its national identity in Egypt and live there peaceably without being assimilated. Israel had come down with all of its livestock with the intention of continuing the ancient family tradition of shepherding flocks and herds. Joseph saw here a real opportunity to keep his family apart from the surrounding culture, as "every shepherd is an abomination to the Egyptians" (46:34). This does not mean that the Egyptians had no livestock but that they disapproved of shepherds, and various reasons have been advanced to explain it. Keepers of livestock tended to be from lower peasant classes; they could well be nomads and were therefore held in suspicion by fixed city dwellers; or they might sacrifice some of the animals that were sacred to the majority of Egyptians. We are given more insight in the book of Exodus where Moses asks Pharaoh to let Israel go and worship him:

> Then Pharaoh called Moses and Aaron and said, "Go, sacrifice to your God within the land." But Moses said, "It would not be right to do so, for the offerings we shall sacrifice to the LORD our God are an abomination to the Egyptians. If we sacrifice offerings abominable to the Egyptians before their eyes, will they not stone us? We must go three days' journey into the wilderness and sacrifice to the LORD our God as he tells us." (Ex. 8:25–27)

This may refer to the fact that in Egypt, the ram was sacred to the gods Amun and Khnum, and, therefore, related animals—lambs and sheep—might well have been regarded in the same way. In light of these cultural and religious practices we can see why Pharaoh would wish to settle Israel in a separate enclave.

In order to achieve this goal, Joseph told his brothers that he would tell Pharaoh the truth about their occupation and that they should do the same when they met Pharaoh and he inquired about their occupations. Eventually Joseph presented five of his brothers to Pharaoh, and the conversation ran as predicted, with the brothers requesting to be allowed to settle in Goshen. Their request was granted by Pharaoh speaking through Joseph. He even asked him to supply herders for his own livestock.

Then came the grand moment when Joseph brought his father Jacob to stand before Pharaoh. It was a remarkable meeting,
where Jacob, unlike his son, did not use the language of subser-
vience or dependence but on the contrary assumed the superior
position and blessed Pharaoh. Jacob had received a great commis-
sion from God and had heard his voice commanding him to go to
Egypt. He would start by doing what his grandfather Abraham
was called to do—be a blessing to the Gentiles. So Jacob blessed
Pharaoh, maybe in part for his role in preserving his son Joseph
and giving Goshen as a safe dwelling place for the family to live.

Pharaoh's question to Jacob is telling: "How many are the days
of the years of your life?" (Gen. 47:8). Pharaoh was concerned, as
his whole nation was concerned, with longevity. This is evidenced
in their practices of seeking to reduce the effects of change and
decay brought about by nature, embalming and mummification
being among them. Powerful as Pharaoh was, he could not control
death.

Jacob admitted his age as 130 and, rather surprisingly, he
openly confessed to Pharaoh that he regarded his many days as
few and evil and less than those of his ancestors. There is a pathos
about this. Jacob had by this point few illusions about himself,
and he felt secure enough in his relationship to God to be able to
admit them to others, even to others wielding great power. Also,
Jacob may have understood Pharaoh's question as an expression
of envy: "I hope I get to your age."[1] His reply could then be understood as saying: "Few and evil have been the days of the years
of my life" (47:9).

Doubtless the memories crowded his mind: his problematic relationships, first with his brother Esau, then with his uncle Laban;
his complex marriages with Leah and Rachel; his problems with
his children; and the long years of mourning over Joseph. Yes,
there was much evil, and the time seemed to have raced by. But

1. Apparently the ideal life span for an Egyptian was 110. Robert Alter, *Genesis: Translation and Commentary* (New York: Norton, 1996), 281.

there was also much for which to be thankful: his family reunited and saved from starvation by his favorite son, the promise of leading a settled existence where the tribe could grow, and the enduring guidance and presence of God.

The meeting was over and Jacob returned to the north where he and his family were settled by Joseph "in the best of the land, the land of Rameses, as Pharaoh had commanded" (47:11). The mention of Rameses is interesting, as it is the name of the city built much later, before the exodus, by Israelite slave labor. Is the writer of Genesis using a deliberate anachronism to indicate the dark days that would come? Kitchen comments on the population mix in this part of Egypt as follows:

> The careful specification (Gen. 39:1) that Joseph's first boss Potiphar was an Egyptian— surely one would *expect* him to be an Egyptian, in Egypt!—suggests that Egyptians were not the sole population in the East Delta around the Pharaoh's residency there. And, archaeologically, for the later Twelfth, all of the Thirteenth, and the Hyksos Dynasties, this is exactly so: there was then a very obvious Canaanite (Middle Bronze Age I–II) component, not only in artefacts such as pottery but also in social usages, such as the placement of burials (by houses) and their arrangements, animal interments, etc. So this small detail may possibly both indicate a basic situation of that age and also hint at its date.[2]

2. K. A. Kitchen, *On the Reliability of the Old Testament* (Grand Rapids, MI: Eerdmans, 2006), 348.

20

The Last Days of
Israel and Joseph

By this stage we may well have lost sight of the fact that Egypt was still in the grip of a famine, and the text now informs us of the strategy that Joseph employed in his ministerial capacity to deal with the economics of food supply.

First, Joseph sold the grain to the Egyptians and the surrounding nations and put the money into Pharaoh's treasury. However, the money supply eventually dried up, and the people clamored for food to keep them alive. Joseph then introduced a barter arrangement whereby people would give him their livestock in exchange for food. That system lasted a year, but eventually they had no more livestock to give. It was all in Pharaoh's possession and most probably given into the custody of Jacob's sons, as Pharaoh had requested. The people then offered the only thing they had left: their land and themselves as serfs to Pharaoh in exchange for food. At this point some manuscripts add that Joseph transferred the rural population to cities, a move that is hard to understand since the land still had to be cultivated and managed. The only exceptions to these policies were the priests, whose land was not taken. They lived on a fixed allowance from Pharaoh.

The result was that ownership of all of the land passed into the hands of Pharaoh, like everything else. Then Joseph, knowing that the famine was in its last stages, introduced a system of supplying seed to the Egyptians, taxing the resultant crop at twenty percent—generous, according to rates in other parts of the then world then and, interestingly enough, the minimum rate at which some countries today set their income tax.

We in the twenty-first century read this with some puzzlement, for Joseph's land management policies had effectively resulted in serfdom. This should not, by the way, be confused with the horrors of the African slave trade. We can see this in the people's reaction to Joseph: "You have saved our lives; may it please my lord, we will be servants to Pharaoh" (Gen. 47:25). Some scholars interpret this as more like tenured farming and think that there are indications that it was not meant to be permanent.

By contrast, Israel in Egypt enjoyed the favor of Joseph's special protection and had all the food they needed. It is not difficult to imagine that this may have sown the seeds of resentment between Egypt and Israel that would culminate in a reversal of these roles, for Israel prospered in the region of Goshen. Such comfort turned the place of exile into a home. That would later lead to many wishing to return to Egypt after Moses had led them out.

Jacob lived in Goshen for seventeen years, exactly the same length of time that Joseph had been with him in Canaan at the beginning. Aware of his impending death, he called Joseph to him and made him promise with an oath not to bury him in Egypt but with Abraham and Isaac in their tomb in Canaan. Jacob's request shows us that he saw the future not in Egypt but in the land promised to Abraham, Isaac, and himself. Even though he had come to Egypt at the call of God, he knew that the stay would only be temporary. He would therefore lay down a marker. By insisting on being buried in Canaan, he would point all subsequent generations to where their future lay. And the first one to whom he would communicate that message was Joseph his son, for he asked Joseph to bury him, thus forcing him to make the journey back to Canaan.

No doubt Jacob thought that Joseph's honoring his request would reestablish a link with the Promised Land and hence with the great Seed Project it represented. The brothers would go as well. Somehow he would get them to set foot in Canaan again. Somehow they would take on God's project once more and bear the burden of Jacob's vision. In effect, Jacob wanted his funeral to precipitate a mini exodus, a harbinger of the greater exodus to come.

Not long after, Jacob succumbed to what was to be his final illness. Joseph was told about it and took his two children, Manasseh and Ephraim, and brought them to Jacob. Jacob spoke first about God appearing to him in the land of Canaan and making a promise to him of many descendants who would have that land as an everlasting possession. Joseph had given Goshen to Jacob as a possession, but it was not to be permanent, as Jacob here pointedly says. Egypt was not the Promised Land.

Jacob then laid claim to Joseph's sons, deliberately naming Ephraim, the youngest, first and then Manasseh; they shall be his even as Reuben and Simeon were. He thus incorporates them into the tribes of Israel with, as Kass points out, the implication that they are no longer Egyptian.[1] Jacob's two grandsons are thereby adopted as his sons. This means that in effect the tribe of Joseph becomes two tribes, Ephraim and Manasseh.

The aged Israel—Jacob—was effectively blind, but he had all his wits about him as is shown by what he did next. He dimly perceived that Joseph's children were present and asked who they were and drew them near to be kissed and hugged. Very movingly Israel said to his son, "I never expected to see your face; and behold, God has let me see your offspring also" (48:11).

---

1. Leon Kass, *The Beginning of Wisdom: Reading Genesis* (New York: Free Press, 2003), 640.

Joseph then carefully positioned the children, Ephraim in his right hand and Manasseh in his left, and led them toward Jacob's left and right hands, respectively. But Jacob crossed his hands, placing his right on Ephraim's head and his left on Manasseh's and proceeded to bless the boys.

Joseph was displeased at his father's action and tried to undo it by taking his father's hand to move it. Jacob stopped him, saying that he knew exactly what he was doing. Both boys were to be great, but the younger was to be greater than the older, mirroring what had happened years before when Jacob, the younger, had gained the greater blessing from Isaac than did Esau his brother.

Then Israel tells his son Joseph that God would be with him and bring him once more into the land of his fathers—indeed he had given Joseph an extra stake in the land above that given to his brothers. Once more, Joseph is left in no doubt that Egypt is not the Promised Land. God will take him out of it.

Jacob's final act was to call all his sons together to hear his farewell address. The speech is in the form of a lengthy poem, replete with metaphorical language that even scholars find difficult to understand. Jacob speaks to each of his sons in turn. Some of what he says is by way of explicit rebuke for past misdeeds; for instance, to the first three sons—Reuben, for sleeping with his father's concubine; Simeon and Levi, for violence. Some is praise, as in the case of Judah, who is represented as the leader to whom the people's obedience will be directed. Joseph is described as a "fruitful bough by a spring; his branches run over the wall" (49:22), and Jacob pronounces on him many blessings from Almighty God, the God of Israel, much more than on any other of his assembled sons.

Joseph is to be exceedingly fruitful, but he is not to be the national leader. That role has been given to Judah. Kass makes the perceptive comment: "Joseph, it appears, had only half understood his youthful 'Egyptian' dream about the sheaves of wheat: his brothers did indeed bow down to him, but only in Egypt. In Israel, the brothers—including Joseph's sons—will be led by

Judah."[2] Jacob ends his farewell oration by making brief reference to Benjamin. He then tells his sons exactly where to bury him and breathes his last.

Joseph wept over his dead father and then commanded his expert embalmers to prepare the body and wrap it in linen—a task that took forty days. This process of mummification was very important in Egyptian culture. Great stress was placed on preserving the dead in lifelike form, as they believed that the survival of the body was necessary for continued existence in the underworld after death. The whole nation of Egypt mourned for seventy days at the death of the father of the man who had saved their nation from starvation.

Joseph finally approached Pharaoh for permission to go to Canaan to bury his father, pointedly adding that he would then return, just in case Pharaoh might think that Joseph was going to use the opportunity to go back to his family roots.

The funeral was an elaborate affair, the largest recorded in Scripture. Not only did all of Jacob's family go up; so also did many dignitaries from Egypt with their chariots and horsemen. It was unheard of in that part of the world, and it stirred up immense interest even in Canaan. They laid Jacob in his ancestral tomb and made their way back to Egypt. One cannot help wondering whether there was a hidden agenda behind the large Egyptian presence at the funeral: to make sure that the economic wunderkind, Joseph, returned to Egypt and did not defect.

Jacob had gone; the family was left without his strong influence. Joseph was by far the most powerful man among the brothers. He operated in a vastly more complex and high-powered world from theirs, and they were dependent on him as benefactor. They began to worry about Joseph's attitude toward them now that Jacob was out of the picture:

When Joseph's brothers saw that their father was dead, they said, "It may be that Joseph will hate us and pay us back for

2. Ibid., 648.

all the evil that we did to him." So they sent a message to
Joseph, saying, "Your father gave this command before he
died: 'Say to Joseph, "Please forgive the transgression of your
brothers and their sin, because they did evil to you."' And
now, please forgive the transgression of the servants of the
God of your father." Joseph wept when they spoke to him.
His brothers also came and fell down before him and said,
"Behold, we are your servants." But Joseph said to them,
"Do not fear, for am I in the place of God? As for you, you
meant evil against me, but God meant it for good, to bring
it about that many people should be kept alive, as they are
today. So do not fear; I will provide for you and your little
ones." Thus he comforted them and spoke kindly to them.
(50:15–21)

Whether Jacob actually said this to the brothers, we do not
know, but they were clearly trying to use his authority, even
though he was dead, to gain leverage with Joseph. Their statement shows clear repentance—they admitted that what they had
done to Joseph was evil, sinful transgression—and they explicitly
asked him to forgive them.

For a final time in this great narrative, Joseph wept, sad, we
can imagine, that his brothers had not grasped the magnanimity
of the forgiveness he had already expressed. And so he once more
explained his view of the whole episode: "You meant evil against
me, but God meant it for good." He recognized the hatred that lay
behind their action, but he was confident that behind it all, there
was the gracious providence of God in bringing about salvation
for starving people. This being the case, they had no need to fear;
nothing would deflect Joseph from continuing to provide for them
and their children.

Joseph's statement shows the delicate but real balance between
God's sovereignty and human responsibility. It reminds us that
the tendency to emphasize one to the exclusion of the other cannot be right.

Joseph spoke kindly and comforted the very men who had spoken to him aggressively and treated him roughly when he was a boy. The family was reconciled.

The fact that, after all this time, the brothers were still nervous and uncertain about the completeness of Joseph's forgiveness was very true to life. How many older people have I met, and some not so old, who believe the gospel and have professed it for years, and yet I sense an unease when I speak with them? Sometimes the problem is that although they would say that God has forgiven them, they cannot fully believe it. There is unfinished business in their hearts, a skeleton in the cupboard, maybe even from the distant past, that troubles them deeply. They have no peace. They are still afraid, particularly of meeting God.

What is the answer? The gospel, actually—how could there be any other? The real problem is often that they have not really grasped the depth and completeness of the forgiveness that Christ offers those who repent and put their trust in him. He died for all of our sins, including those hidden in the disturbing closet of memory. What we are required to do as Christians is, first, to realize that the Lord is perfectly aware of what we have done; and, second, to confess to him those things that still bother us; and finally to trust what he promises as explained by the apostle John:

> If we say we have no sin, we deceive ourselves, and the truth
> is not in us. If we confess our sins, he is faithful and just to
> forgive us our sins and to cleanse us from all unrighteousness.
> If we say we have not sinned, we make him a liar, and his word
> is not in us. (1 John 1:8–10)

The tribe multiplied, and Joseph grew older and neared death. He called his brothers and said his last words to them:

> "I am about to die, but God will visit you and bring you up
> out of this land to the land that he swore to Abraham, to Isaac,
> and to Jacob." Then Joseph made the sons of Israel swear,

saying, "God will surely visit you, and you shall carry up my bones from here." So Joseph died, being 110 years old. They embalmed him, and he was put in a coffin in Egypt. (Gen. 50:24–26)

Joseph believed that God would one day fulfill his promise to Abraham, Isaac, and Jacob. Hence, Joseph's last request to his tribe was that when that exodus happened, they would take his bones with them so that his last resting place would be with the patriarchs in the Promised Land.

The New Testment refers to these last words of Joseph as evidence of his faith in God: "By faith Joseph, at the end of his life, made mention of the exodus of the Israelites and gave directions concerning his bones" (Heb. 11:22). Yes, he was embalmed in Egyptian fashion and put in a coffin in Egypt. Yet by insisting that his remains should one day be taken by Israel to the Promised Land, Joseph demonstrated that he knew that the future did not lie in Egypt. He knew that his nation would one day leave Egypt and carry forward the great Seed Project that had started with Abraham and would keep going until the Seed himself, God incarnate, would come to planet earth and effect salvation for the world and so bring in the great blessing promised to the patriarchs.

The life and experience of Joseph form an important pointer in that direction. God raised up Joseph, an Israelite, as a savior of the world. Yet he was initially rejected by his people, the rest of Israel, and remained "dead" to them for years. As we noted earlier, the first Christian martyr, Stephen, points this out in his powerful speech to the Sanhedrin in Jerusalem and compares the patriarchs' attitude to Joseph to Israel's rejection of Moses and, most importantly, to their rejection of the Savior of the world, the Messiah, Jesus the Lord.

We can see a pattern in biblical history. Every time God raised up a savior, the nation rejected him, and the savior suffered before he was recognized for what God had chosen him to be. The path was one of suffering first and glory afterward. The apostle Peter says that this is a path predicted by the prophets as the way in which Christ would bring salvation:

> Concerning this salvation, the prophets who prophesied about the grace that was to be yours searched and inquired carefully, inquiring what person or time the Spirit of Christ in them was indicating when he predicted the sufferings of Christ and the subsequent glories. (1 Pet. 1:10–11)

At the close of his letter Peter gently applies this fact in order to encourage Christian believers who are suffering or about to suffer for their faith in Christ: "And after you have suffered a little while, the God of all grace, who has called you to his eternal glory in Christ, will himself restore, confirm, strengthen, and establish you" (5:10).

Joseph first suffered and then entered into the glory of high office in Egypt. At a far higher level, Jesus suffered and entered into the glory of heaven. Joseph knew that Egypt was not heaven; his request about his bones proved that. But Joseph is in heaven because of the path that Jesus followed.

It is interesting to know that in later history, some Jews floated the idea that there would be two messiahs, Mashiach ben Yosef and Mashiach ben David, descended, respectively, from Joseph and David. Some believed that the former would be killed in the battle against evil, and the latter would appear to avenge his death and bring in the messianic kingdom.

But there were not to be two messiahs—only one, Yeshua, Jesus, of the tribe of Judah, who would fulfill both roles, to suffer and die for human salvation and to rise again and ascend to heaven from where he will one day come to rule.

Joseph was rejected by his brothers, treated as dead, but he went on and eventually became instrumental in saving many Gentiles. His brothers then arrived in Egypt for food, and when he saw evidence of their repentance Joseph forgave them and revealed himself to them. And at a deeper level and on a larger scale, when Jesus died and the Jews, by and large, rejected the gospel, the apostles turned to the Gentiles, who have come to trust Christ in large numbers through the centuries. Regarding this Paul writes: "Now I am speaking to you Gentiles. Inasmuch then as I am an apostle to the Gentiles, I magnify my ministry in order somehow to make my fellow Jews jealous, and thus save some of them. For if their rejection means the reconciliation of the world, what will their acceptance mean but life from the dead?" (Rom. 11:13–15).

Paul goes on to say that that day will undoubtedly come:

> Lest you be wise in your own sight, I do not want you to be unaware of this mystery, brothers: a partial hardening has come upon Israel, until the fullness of the Gentiles has come in. And in this way all Israel will be saved, as it is written, "The Deliverer will come from Zion, he will banish ungodliness from Jacob"; "and this will be my covenant with them when I take away their sins." As regards the gospel, they are enemies for your sake. But as regards election, they are beloved for the sake of their forefathers. For the gifts and the calling of God are irrevocable. (Rom. 11:25–29)

When we look at the complexities of the life of Joseph and then compare them with God's larger dealings in history, we begin to understand a little of what Paul meant when he concluded:

> Oh, the depth of the riches and wisdom and knowledge of God! How unsearchable are his judgments and how inscrutable his ways! (Rom. 11:33)

Appendix 1

Major Divisions of Ancient Egyptian History

Predynastic Period c. 5500–3200
Protodynastic Period 3200–3100
Early Dynastic (Dynasties 1 and 2) 3100–2686
1st hieroglyphs Step pyramid built at Saqqara
Old Kingdom (3rd–6th Dynasties) 2686–2181
Great Pyramid at Giza
Great Sphinx
Step Pyramid of Djoser
Pyramids of Giza
First Intermediate Period (7th–11th Dynasties) *2181–2055*
Memphis rules Egypt in the north and Thebes in the south
Middle Kingdom (11th–13th Dynasties) *2055–1650*
Egypt reunited and conquers Lower Nubia
Second Intermediate Period (14th–17th Dynasties) *1650–1550*
The Hyksos
New Kingdom (18th–20th Dynasties) *1550–1069*
Empire in the Near East, Hatshepsut, Akhenaten, Tutankha-
    men and Ramessid Period
Abu Simbel
Amarna

King Tut
Nefertiti
Tutankhamun's Tomb
Third Intermediate Period (21st–24th Dynasties) 1059–747
Nubians conquer Egypt
Late Period (25th–30th Dynasties plus 3 Persian kings) 747–332
Assyrians, Persians conquer Egypt
Greco-Roman Period 332 BC–AD 395
Ptolemaic 332–330
Greeks conquer Egypt, Rosetta Stone, Cleopatra
Roman 30 BC–AD 395

General Index

Abraham, 15, 16, 27; binding of Isaac, 31–32, 203; as blessing to Gentiles, 209; covenant with, 204; faith of, 28, 29; gone to Egypt, 163; promise to, 28
Adam and Eve, temptation of, 125, 127
adultery, 126, 130
African slave trade, 212
Akhenaten, 148
Amarna, 110
Amenemhat I, 107
Amenhotep IV, 110
Amish community, 172, 180–81
Amun, 109
Ananias and Sapphira, 102
anger, 166
anxiety, 120–21
Asenath, 158–60
Asher, 45
assimilation into heathen culture, 202, 207
Aten, 110
atheism, 16, 23; judgment on, 25; morality of, 19
atomism, 16

Babel, 27
baker, dream of, 10, 138–39, 141, 149
Bard, Kathryn, 105–6

Beersheva, 203
Benjamin, 45, 68, 80, 160, 166–67, 182, 184, 185–88, 215
Bernhardt, Mindy, 175
Bethel, 35, 65-67
Bilhah, 68
bitterness, 183
blood of Christ, 86
Brezina, Timothy, 175
Brothers Karamazov (Dostoyevsky), 19
brothers of Joseph, 202; anger about Joseph's dream, 90–91; bow to Joseph in Egypt, 164, 188, 214; go down to Egypt to buy grain, 163–64; hatred of Joseph, 74, 79
Browning, Robert, 154

Cain and Abel, 24
Campbell, Bradley, 129–30, 132–33
Canaan, 11, 62, 65, 75, 163, 212–13, 215
Canaanites, 67
carelessness, 153
character, 123
child abuse, 131
Christmas, 156
Christophanies, 53
circumcision, 63
clothes, as false evidence, 130–31
confession and forgiveness, 99

Scripture Index